hazardous
to
our
wealth

hazardous to our wealth

economic policies in the 1980s

Frank Ackerman

south end press

boston ma

contents

tables

acknowledgements

A number of people helped make this book possible. Kathy Moore, Arthur MacEwan and David Kotz offered valuable editorial suggestions on earlier drafts. Dick Cluster helped produce the statistical analysis of inflation presented in Table 6. John Schall of South End Press worked preposterously long hours to get this book done promptly.

This book began as a second edition of my earlier book, *Reaganomics: Rhetoric vs. Reality.* Large sections of *Reaganomics* are certainly recognizable here, appropriately updated; but there are several major changes which give this book own unique identity. When the earlier book was written, Reaganomics was just beginning; much of it was still in the realm of plans and proposals. This book examines the economic results of Ronald Reagan's first three years in office.

Moreover, the discussion of Reaganomics here is organized around the contrast among rival conservative theories—supply-side economics, military Keynesianism, and monetarism. At least the latter two will be important well beyond Ronald Reagan's tenure in the White House. Finally, this book is not just about Reaganomics, but about the wider debate over economic policies for the 1980s. So it also includes a discussion of the leading alternatives—neo-liberalism and "economic democracy."

Portions of this book have previously appeared in *Dollars & Sense*, in *Democratic Left* (the magazine of the Democratic Socialists of America), and in the *National Catholic Reporter.* I owe a particular word of thanks to the members of *Dollars & Sense*: I was on the staff of the magazine for eight years, and developed many of my ideas about the economy and how to write about it while working there. Sentences and paragraphs borrowed from *D & S* articles will be found here and there in the following pages. If you would like to read a magazine about the economy, written from a point of view similar to this book, contact *Dollars & Sense* at 38 Union Square, Room 14, Somerville, MA 02143.

chapter 1

the
way
the
world
doesn't
work

How is it possible to raise defense spending, cut income taxes, and balance the budget, all at the same time?...
"We've got to figure out a way to make (that question) fit into a plausible policy path over the next three years,"
Stockman said. "Actually, it isn't all that hard to do..."

"The whole thing is premised on faith," Stockman explained. "On a belief about how the world works."
—William Greider,
"The Education of David Stockman"[1]

Ask yourself whether you are better or worse off than you were four years ago, said Ronald Reagan. It was the most memorable, and most successful, question of the 1980 campaign. Millions of people answered when they voted, not so much for the new as against the old. The 1970s had been a decade of quite dramatic failure for traditional economic policies — more than enough reason, it seemed, to try a new belief about how the world works.

Yet the question persists. Ask yourself whether you are better or worse off, Democratic candidates repeated in the depths of the Reagan recession in 1982. The question will remain with us until the economic crisis has been solved. For the U.S. economy

1

has done much better before, and can do much better again. Reaganomics is the first new departure to be tried, but likely not the last.

The economic failures of the 1970s and 1980s contrasted sharply with the preceding era of success. Back in the "good old days" of the 1950s and 1960s, incomes, on average, climbed at a fairly steady pace. Inflation was all but unknown, and spells of high unemployment were brief.

Such times are long gone. The purchasing power of the average worker's take-home pay reached an all-time high in 1972, then fell 16% in the following ten years. Average family incomes roughly kept pace with inflation in the 1970s, but only because more and more families added second or third wage-earners. Inflation, interest rates and unemployment reached levels that would have been called catastrophic in earlier years. Throughout the 1970s, Republican and Democratic administrations alike seemed powerless to reverse our declining fortunes.

In 1981 the new administration set out to change all that. Within a month of taking office, Reagan announced his four-part "program for economic recovery": civilian budget cuts and military buildup; tax cuts; rollback of federal regulations; and monetary policies that would cause high interest rates. The first stages of this program were adopted with astonishing speed, much to the delight of some people. Generals and military contractors rejoiced at the shift of funds from civilian agencies to the Pentagon. Upper-income taxpayers enjoyed the particular biases of the Reagan tax cut. Corporate polluters breathed more freely thanks to deregulation.

Others were less satisfied. In the twelve months following the passage of the "Economic Recovery Tax Act of 1981" (as it was officially named), the ranks of the unemployed swelled by more than three million. Production and investment, as well as employment, headed down under the initial onslaught of Reaganomics. The President proclaimed his support for a constitutional amendment to require a balanced budget—as if unaware that his own policies were driving the budget deficit to record levels. Budget Director David Stockman quickly lost his faith that it would be easy to find a "plausible policy path"; by the middle of 1981 he had already concluded, "There was a certain dimension of our theory that was unrealistic..."

That unrealistic dimension includes the entire analysis of

what went wrong in the 1970s. Despite some dramatic reversals in specific policies, the Reagan team held fast to its fundamental economic belief: private enterprise will work wonders if only the government leaves it alone. If the problem is government interference, then the solution is to cut back everything (well, almost everything) the government does. Perhaps if the Reaganites were right about the problem, they would be right about the solution. But the world doesn't work that way.

Although the expanding role of government is, of course, involved in the economic problems which emerged in the 1970s, that is far from the whole story. A look at the real causes of our prolonged crisis will reveal the reasons why Reaganomics has been no solution at all for almost all of us.

The economic problems of recent years are best understood by contrast with the less troubled era just after World War II. The growth and prosperity of much of the 1950s and 1960s rested on five favorable conditions: U.S. international power; abundant supplies of cheap oil; the growth of the auto/highway/suburb complex; the informal truce between business and labor; and the particular nature of government intervention in the economy. Changes in all five areas in the late 1960s and early 1970s led to "stagflation"—slow growth, unemployment and inflation.

Traditional economic policies clearly failed to cope with these problems in the 1970s. Reaganomics has offered only a very partial, biased response to the causes of stagflation, and has only a provided very partial, biased cure. So the search continues for more adequate answers to the ongoing economic crisis.

Once upon a time

The map of the route to crisis can begin at a point of undisputed success. We came out on top in World War II, economically as well as militarily. As the only major industrial nation to escape wartime destruction, the United States was in a position of unchallenged worldwide power after 1945. This was the first of the conditions allowing the decades of postwar prosperity.

The products of U.S. factories and farms were in demand around the world, leading to a steady trade surplus (that is, our exports were greater than our imports) through the mid-1960s. U.S. foreign aid programs strengthened our trading partners, allowing them to buy more from us. For instance, the Marshall Plan helped revive wartorn European economies and reintegrate them with ours. As well as being our top export market, Europe soon became the fastest-growing area of foreign investment by U.S. corporations, returning an ever-growing stream of profits to this country.[2]

There were other places besides Europe where the U.S. newly asserted its power. Our government moved rapidly to replace British and French influence in many Third World countries. Networks of aid, anti-communist alliances and military bases circled the globe. In the extreme, we resorted to direct interventions: CIA-sponsored coups in Iran in 1953 and Guatemala in 1954, landings of the Marines in Lebanon in 1958 and the Dominican Republic in 1965, and the unsuccessful Bay of Pigs invasion of Cuba in 1962, to name the most blatant cases. Our increasingly multinational corporations followed the flag overseas, gaining access to Third World markets, low-wage labor and cheap raw materials. Again, a rising tide of profits flowed homeward as U.S. business expanded abroad.

A massive military apparatus was created to defend this informal empire against real or imagined threats—often against nationalist movements in the more impoverished provinces of the "Free World" itself. And in the Cold War climate of the 1950s, few questions were asked about the need for military spending. After the Korean War, both direct military employment and weapons production remained higher than ever before in peacetime, boosting the rate of economic growth.

New industries sprang up as spin-offs from the military. Civilian aircraft and airlines became possible because the Air Force had developed the planes and trained so many pilots. The Pentagon bought more than half the computers and a third of the semiconductors produced throughout the 1950s and early 1960s, helping to launch these crucial industries.[3] Nuclear energy, which at the time looked like a promising new technology for the future, was a byproduct of the nuclear weapons program. Not only U.S. international power, but also the arsenal which supported it, seemed to be good for business.

Among the treasures that multinational corporations brought back from their foreign adventures, none was more important than petroleum. The years after World War II were the years of cheap oil, from both foreign and domestic sources—the second of the conditions on which U.S. prosperity was based. New oil fields in Venezuela, Texas and the Middle East, almost all under American control, flooded the industrial world, driving out fuels such as coal and reshaping manufacturing and transportation.

Entire industries owe their existence or their dominant technologies to the former availability of cheap oil. As long as the price of petroleum was low, it made good business sense to use it extravagantly (by today's standards), to replace other materials and fuels with it. Thus petrochemical industries such as plastics and synthetic fibers used petroleum as their basic raw material. Agribusiness reorganized the farm with oil-powered machinery and oil-based fertilizers and pesticides. The rise of energy-guzzling air transportation, and the decline of energy-efficient railroads, could only have happened in a society that had liquid fuel to burn.

Cheap oil also made it possible for our lives to be transformed by the boom in automobiles, highways, suburbs and a host of related industries—the third condition underlying postwar prosperity. At the end of World War II there were 26 million cars on the roads, less than one for every five people; by 1973 there were 102 million, or one for every two people.[4] The creation of interstate highways and urban expressways allowed the ever-widening sprawl of suburbs and shopping centers, and the accompanying growth in construction and consumer goods. The value of new construction, corrected for inflation, grew by 4.3% per year from 1947 to 1965.[5] Factories as well as people moved to new suburban locations, as trucks replaced railroads in freight transportation. The strong unions of the day—the building trades, teamsters, auto, rubber and steel workers—were those whose members made and moved the products required for the suburban transformation.

As basic industries expanded, the relations between employers and unions became calmer than ever before or since—the fourth of the bases of prosperity. Management grudgingly accepted unionization as a fact of life; unions purged their most militant leaders in the late 1940s, as McCarthyism and "red scares" swept the nation. In place of the angry confrontations that accompanied the rise of industrial unions in the 1930s and 1940s, both management and labor settled down to a predictable routine of collective bargaining by the 1950s.

The mystique of the marketplace, of business yearning to grow as soon as government gets out of the way, has become newly popular in the Reagan years. Contrary to this view, active government "interference" was one of the major conditions stimulating the post-World War II expansion. Federal government spending, a mere 3% of gross national product (GNP) in 1929, never fell below 14% after 1945. Income taxes, previously paid only by the rich, were extended to almost everyone during World War II; after the war, the broadened tax and the expanded government role which it made possible both survived. State and local government spending rose as well, and total government spending at all levels averaged 27% of GNP in the 1950s and early 1960s.[6]

With memories of the 1930s' depression still fresh, the belief became widespread that the government should step in to prevent recessions—or to speed up recovery when recessions did occur. The brief downturns of the era have been described as "hiccups between linked booms"; prompt increases in government spending helped ensure that they became nothing worse.

Moreover, in the early postwar years, government spending was heavily concentrated in programs that were attractive to business. In 1955, the military accounted for 32% of all public spending, federal, state and local; highways took 6%, and construction contracts for schools and other public buildings absorbed another several percentage points.

From the corporate point of view, military spending is the ideal government activity. In addition to whatever protection of foreign trade and investment it may provide, the Pentagon does not compete with private industry. On the contrary, it offers lucrative contracts to aerospace and other firms, and stimulates the creation of spin-off industries as well. Most government construction projects likewise provide juicy contracts, do not compete with private business, and may even (as with highways) lay the groundwork for private-sector prosperity.

The height of optimism about the government's ability to manage the economy was reached by the liberal advisors to the Kennedy and Johnson administrations in the 1960s. Presiding over the last long stretch of postwar prosperity, and over a rapid expansion in the size and role of the public sector, they claimed that they could "fine-tune" the economy to a desired level of employment and growth. But the grounds for their optimism, never terribly secure to begin with, were rapidly crumbling by the time they left office.

How the end began

An impressive constellation of circumstances powered the postwar boom. But none of them were eternal. Many of them were unavoidably eroded by the very fact of twenty years of prosperity. In each of the five areas just described, changes appeared in the late 1960s and early 1970s. It is these changing conditions which caused the economic problems of recent years. It is these changing conditions which Reaganomics has done such a poor job of addressing, and which any newer economic alternative will confront as well.

Internationally, the wartime destruction of Europe and Japan was clearly temporary. U.S. trade and investment only hastened their return to the status of serious competitors. And with lower wages, newer plants and leaner management styles, they were serious competitors indeed. Suddenly the U.S. was no longer the only source of manufactured goods in the world. The U.S. trade surplus peaked in 1964 and then fell to a deficit, the first in the twentieth century, by 1971. The balance of trade has become even worse since then. By the late 1970s, our imports exceeded exports by more than $2 billion per month. The vanishing trade surplus has meant fewer markets for U.S.-made goods, fewer jobs, and slower growth of the U.S. economy.

At about the same time, U.S. power in the Third World was meeting with decisive military defeat in Vietnam. In the wake of that war, liberation movements also came to power in Angola, Mozambique, Guinea-Bissau, Zimbabwe and Nicaragua. Each of these would, in an earlier time, have been met by the Marines. But in the 1970s, defeat on the battlefield and domestic opposition to war eliminated the option of intervention. Gloomy noises about the tides of world history were heard for a time in Washington and Wall Street.

It is not so coincidental that the end of cheap oil came in the same period. Back in the old days, the U.S. did not permit such impudence. In 1953 the nationalist government of Iran, which had taken control of that country's oil, was overthrown by the CIA. By 1973, though, when the first big price hike by OPEC (the Organization of Petroleum Exporting Countries) occurred, another U.S. military intervention was politically impossible. The rise of OPEC may be counted among the indirect effects of the war in Vietnam.

There was more to OPEC's triumph than just the anti-interventionist climate of the times. The world oil market was also quite favorable to the producing nations. By 1970 both U.S. and Venezuelan oil output had peaked and begun to decline, leaving consumers increasingly reliant on a handful of Middle Eastern countries. Then a brief worldwide economic boom in 1972-73 sent prices of other raw materials soaring. OPEC oil ministers undoubtedly noticed these trends and seized on the first plausible excuse, the Middle East war in late 1973, to quadruple the price of their oil. But even with such a favorable market position, it is unlikely that OPEC would have tried anything so bold in the days when U.S. "gunboat diplomacy" reigned supreme.

The energy price explosions of the last decade have flattened oil-intensive industries. The combination of high oil prices and low consumer incomes has pushed major airlines to the brink of bankruptcy (and occasionally beyond), caused farm failures and foreclosures at rates reminiscent of the 1930s, and dimmed the growth prospects of many petrochemicals. The massive U.S. investment in oil-hungry industries made economic sense only at pre-crisis prices. At today's energy prices, it is unlikely that the present levels of replacing natural materials with plastics and synthetics, or ground transportation with airplanes, or even railroads with cars and trucks, would ever have developed.

Growth based on autos, highways and suburbs had built-in limits, which were being felt even before the oil crisis. When all major cities are tied to one another with ribbons of concrete and ringed with suburbs and shopping malls, when every garage contains a car and many hold two, there is simply no room for more. Shifting patterns of population and industry may mean that construction continues around some Sunbelt cities or "high-tech" enclaves. But overall the pace of growth is far below the heyday of highways and suburbanization.

The value of new construction, corrected for inflation, rose by an average of only 0.5% from 1965 to 1978, far below its earlier 4.3% rate. And after 1978 the bottom fell out of the construction business entirely. High gasoline prices make the most remote suburbs and longest commutes even less attractive than before, dampening the outer reaches of suburban sprawl.

By the end of the 1960s, the truce between capital and labor was under attack from both sides. Business, feeling the decline in profits as the crisis began, sought to speed up workers, and to hold the line on wage increases. Workers, buoyed by a long period of high employment and steadily rising wages, were initially in a strong position to resist. Wildcat strikes spread throughout industry; debates about worker alienation moved out of sociology textbooks and into the daily news. Growing numbers of businesses moved to non-union areas of the country, or even overseas. An increasingly hostile, confrontational era of labor relations was beginning.

Finally, the nature of government intervention in the economy was also changing. For a while after World War II, most spending by the federal government was justified in Cold War terms. The interstate highways were supposed to facilitate rapid movement of troops and weapons in case of invasion. Even the school lunch program was said to boost military preparedness, since so many potential soldiers had flunked their physical due to nutritional deficiencies in World War II.

But as the Russians persisted year after year in their stubborn refusal to invade Western Europe, Cold War politics gradually receded. The Pentagon's budget, though massive, barely kept up with inflation from 1955 to 1980 (the peak years of Vietnam war spending excepted). Other areas were expanding much faster. The two leading growth areas in public spending were retirement benefits and education; a host of smaller health and welfare programs were being created or expanded as well.

The growth of social programs has a contradictory effect on business. On the one hand, companies are happy to have a healthier, better educated workforce. Unemployment benefits encourage experienced workers to stick around instead of leaving town during layoffs. Social Security checks reduce the demand for private pensions.

On the other hand, this is an area where businessmen definitely find it possible to have too much of a good thing. In the 1960s and early 1970s the civil rights, anti-poverty and other movements forced the rapid increase of government benefits and services. The sheer size of social welfare spending, the momentum of growth and the grassroots political initiative involved came to threaten corporate stability. Any income that people receive without working reduces their dependence on employers, and the trend seemed to be toward more and more non-wage income becoming available to the poor. Budget cuts were almost impossible since benefits came to be viewed, and often legally defined, as rights to which people were entitled.

Under the impact of these changes, government spending rose more rapidly in the 1960s than before. The combined total of federal, state and local budgets climbed from 27% of GNP in the early 1960s to 32% in the early 1970s. (This figure did not rise any further, though; it was about the same in the late 1970s.)

The point is not that a magic number had been reached, that 27% of GNP had been okay but 32% somehow broke the bank. Indeed, private enterprise manages to thrive in Western European nations where public spending is routinely well above 32% of GNP. Rather, the problem was that the surge in spending was accompanied by a shift toward areas which business found less profitable and less controllable. The strength of anti-war sentiment held down both the size and the duration of military spending in Vietnam and then put the lid back on the Pentagon budget for the 1970s—allowing social programs to absorb an increasing share of the budget. By 1978 the military accounted for only 14% of all government spending and highways only 3%.

In short, government spending was shifting in a direction which was more helpful to many people, but less advantageous to business. At about the same time, U.S. international power was waning, energy was becoming expensive, the suburban boom was stalling, and conflict between management and labor was heating up again. These are the changes that account for the stagflation of the 1970s, for the failure of traditional economic policy in that decade, and for the failure of Reaganomics in the 1980s as well.

The Reagan revolution

How did the Reagan administration address these fundamental economic problems? For three of the problems, they offered depressing or dangerous solutions; for the other two, they apparently did not understand the questions.

In response to the decline of U.S. power abroad, Reagan launched his massive military buildup. However, the world has changed so much that no amount of rearmament will recreate the position of strength the U.S. possessed before 1965. The drift into Vietnam-style military intervention in Central America is actively opposed by such major allies as France and Mexico. Reagan's nuclear saber-rattling has sparked a peace movement of unprecedented size, both here and in Europe. Getting tough with the Russians will not whip either Europe or the Third World back into line, although Ronald Reagan and the rest of us could easily die trying. And even complete success in projecting U.S. military power around the world would not cure our trade deficit. For that key economic problem, Reaganomics offers only the cruel hope that lower wages will eventually make U.S. products more competitive with imports.

When it comes to energy, Reagan has always been oblivious to the high cost, in both dollars and environmental damage, of his chosen policy of deregulating domestic oil, coal and gas production. The satisfaction of paying the same high prices for domestic energy sources instead of Middle Eastern oil will do little for the consumers and industries who are stuck with the high fuel bills—and with the dirty air and water. Elsewhere in the energy wars, the administration apparently has missed the obituaries for the nuclear power industry, published almost monthly in the business press. While utilities are happy to defend existing and partially completed nukes, they are not about to throw good money after bad by actually ordering new ones. In addition, Reagan has undone what little Carter had achieved in promoting energy conservation and alternative energy development.

The stagnation of autos, highways, suburbs and related areas such as steel and trucking—indeed the very notion that a whole set of once-strong heavy industries are declining,and not much is replacing them—seems to have floated right past the Reagan White House. The concept of a conscious policy for reindustrialization scarcely enters the rhetoric of Reaganomics, let alone the reality. As Congressman Gerry Studds said in a different context (he was criticizing military aid to El Salvador), "No one is going to accuse the current leadership of being either the best or the brightest."[7]

In the conflict between capital and labor, Reaganomics has unambiguously chosen sides. One way to restore profit levels is to crush the union movement, to tip the balance of power in the workplace decisively toward management. And what better way to do that could be imagined than a massive recession, making once-powerful unions desperate enough to surrender their past gains? As a further lesson to workers everywhere, our president demolished the air traffic controllers union (PATCO) in 1981, for daring to strike.

Attacking the changing nature of government is of course what Reagan likes best. Was the past shift from military to civilian spending unprofitable for business? Fear not, help is on the way. In fact, reorienting some of civilian manufacturing toward weapons production is the closest thing to an industrial policy that Reagan has come up with. Have government services and income supports made workers too independent, too capable of resisting wage cuts in recessions? There is good news for employers on this front, too, as one federal program after another has been forced to wither away.

Thus Reaganomics turned out to be militarily dangerous, socially cruel, and industrially short-sighted. It is a far cry from the brave new policies and glowing results that were promised on the campaign trail back in 1980. The search for alternative economic policies for the 1980s is by no means over.

New theories: not one, but three

Even in the earlier era of growth, the progress of the economy was never perfectly smooth. There were ups and downs in production and employment, through relatively more ups and fewer downs than in recent years. The claim that the economy could be "fine-tuned" to a desired level of employment has never been borne out in reality. Still, at least crude tuning of the volume of economic activity did seem to be within the government's reach.

The theory justifying government management of the economy was first developed by John Maynard Keynes. Writing in the depths of the Great Depression, Keynes argued that there was no reason to think that the private sector of the economy could achieve full employment on its own. Under many circumstances, private spending would be insufficient to put everyone to work — particularly when, for whatever reason, businessmen were not spending much for investment.

If the government wanted to cure unemployment, it could use two principal remedies: fiscal policy and monetary policy. Fiscal policy meant either increasing government spending directly, or cutting taxes to allow an increase in private spending. Monetary policy, carried out by the Federal Reserve System, meant manipulating the nation's banks in ways that lowered interest rates and increased the availability of loans. This would encourage business borrowing for investment, and consumer borrowing to buy homes and cars. Similarly, if the government wanted to decrease spending and employment, it could use restrictive fiscal and monetary policies: cutting government spending, raising taxes, raising interest rates, and making loans harder to get.

The Keynesian approach to economic policy was widely accepted among economists from the 1940s through the early 1970s. However, maintaining high employment was not the only goal of public policy. The government was also expected to combat the threat of inflation. Unfortunately, the two goals appeared to be contradictory. There was said to be a "trade-off" between inflation and unemployment. When more people are out of work, wages and prices are supposed to rise more slowly; with progress toward full employment, wages and prices shoot up more rapidly. A graph of this relationship is enshrined in the literature of economics as the "Phillips curve."

The trade-off theory is based on changes in the bargaining strength of capital and labor. When unemployment is very low, employed workers are secure in the knowledge that they are hard to replace. Their bargaining position relative to their employers is strong and they are often able to win large wage gains and other concessions. Businesses pass on most or all of these increased labor costs in the form of higher prices.

When unemployment is high, on the other hand, employed workers are easy to replace, their bargaining position is weak and large gains by labor are rare. Businesses have lower cost increases to pass on. And with consumer incomes down due to unemployment, it's not a great time for raising prices anyway. Thus prosperity causes inflation, and recession stops it.

The goal of economic policy, then, was to find and maintain the perfect amount of unemployment. Too much was clearly undesirable, and too little would provoke inflation. Garbed in varying jargons, this idea was the basis of Republican and Democratic policy alike for decades.

The dismal economic record of the 1970s led many people to conclude that the theory of the inflation-unemployment trade-off was no longer valid. After all, we seemed to be enjoying the worst of both. Yet at any one time unemployment does slow inflation. The 1974-75 recession, in which the official unemployment rate briefly hit 9%, brought the rate of inflation down from 12% in 1974 to 5% in 1976. Similarly, Reagan's recession has driven down the rate of inflation from 12%-13% in 1979-80 to 4% in 1982, though this time stopping double-digit inflation led to a prolonged bout of double-digit unemployment.[8] (For a more detailed look at inflation during these two recessions, see pp. 138-141 below.)

But if the inflation-unemployment trade-off still works at any one time, it appears to work ever more painfully as time goes on. More and more unemployment is needed to achieve the same reduction in inflation. The situation may be compared to pumping the water out of an increasingly leaky boat. On any day the pump still works, but every day it takes more pumping to achieve the same reduction in wetness. In the language of economists, the terms of the trade-off between pumping effort and wetness, between unemployment and inflation, are worsening.

The worsening terms of the trade-off result in several ways from the forces that ended postwar prosperity, as discussed above. The oil crisis, for instance, has meant that OPEC and the oil companies have much greater power to raise prices. Any given level of unemployment, therefore, is now accompanied by higher and faster-rising energy prices than it would have been before 1973.

The very fact of stagnation, the slowing of economic growth, itself causes an increase in inflation. In the traditional metaphor, when the pie is growing, everyone can have a bigger slice with little conflict. But when the pie stops growing, any increase must come at someone else's expense. The "size of the pie," measured by GNP per worker (corrected for inflation), grew by an annual average of 2.6% from 1947 to 1966, but only 0.9% from 1966 to 1980.

In the years of faster growth, both labor and capital came to expect that they could win steadily rising incomes; when growth began to sputter, the continuing demands for higher wages and profits came into conflict, adding to inflationary pressures. Consumer prices climbed by an annual average of only 2% from 1947 to 1966, compared to 8% from 1966 to 1980. The inflationary spiral was begun by deficit financing of the Vietnam war in the late 1960s, but continued well after war spending declined, in part due to the clashing expectations of labor and capital.

It was not only the memories of growth in past years that

created expectations of rising wages and prices. The changing role of the government reinforced those expectations. Growing public expenditures on programs such as unemployment compensation, food stamps and welfare enabled workers to accept brief layoffs rather than taking any available job, no matter how poorly paid. More broadly, the government's evident commitment to preventing major depressions encouraged workers and employers to resist wage and price cuts in recessions. If the return of prosperity is known to be right around the corner, a temporary drop in employment or sales has little effect on wages and prices. The more often that recessions turned out to be nothing serious, the less effective they became in scaring people.

The situation was quite different in the nineteenth century, when such amenities as unemployment benefits and government attempts to promote full employment were virtually unknown. Superficially it was a century of success in controlling inflation: prices were lower in 1900 than in 1800. Nineteenth-century prices rose rapidly, especially during wars, but fell again during the frequent panics and depressions.

In an old-fashioned depression, the trade-off was ruthlessly effective. Fear of starvation forced workers to bid their wages lower and lower, and the collapse of consumer markets forced companies to slash their prices. Few people today would advocate more frequent depressions as a method of price control. But it should not be forgotten that it is the principal method that has worked in the past.

Although the inflation-unemployment trade-off was steadily worsening in the 1970s, it still worked after a fashion. Throughout the decade the Nixon, Ford and Carter administrations periodically lunged into recessions when the pressure of inflation looked too severe. Even a very leaky boat can be temporarily pumped dry, with enough effort. But floundering along on yesterday's answers was becoming increasingly ineffective and unpopular. The rising tide of stagflation seemed to be swamping not only the trade-off mechanism, but also the entire Keynesian faith in the government's ability to manage the economy. A drastic new approach was called for.

Ronald Reagan was popular in 1980 because he offered a new economic policy. He claimed he could restore economic growth, stop inflation without recession, and make everyone better off at once. On closer inspection, Reaganomics turned out to involve not one, but three sometimes contradictory approaches to managing the economy. Only one is actually new; all three, though, have been applied with impressive speed and thoroughness, if not success.

The first, the novelty item of the 1980 campaign, is supply-side economics. Its theory is the subject of Chapter 2. A new way of thinking and talking about the economy, often presented as part of a grand conservative fantasy about society as a whole, leads to a striking policy proposal: cut taxes and government regulations fast enough and everyone, the federal treasury included, will soon be richer than before. So far we have had the supply-siders' tax cut (discussed in Chapter 3) and much of their deregulatory agenda (Chapter 4); the promised miracle of wealth, unfortunately, has been postponed.

The second approach may be called military Keynesianism. While the very concept of government spending to create jobs and revive the economy was banished from the garden of Reaganomics, the Pentagon crept back in to nibble at (indeed, to gulp down) the forbidden fruit of taxpayers' dollars. Though justified in apocalyptic Cold War terms, and hence exempt from the ordinary prohibitions on wasteful government programs, military spending has played the same Keynesian role of job creation under Reagan as it did under any other administration. It is discussed in Chapter 5.

The third approach is monetarism, a favorite of traditional conservatives. Monetarists present an intricate critique of Keynesian policies, and propose instead a steady, slow rate of growth for the nation's supply of money (even though that will often drive interest rates sky-high), and as little government spending as possible. Chapter 6 deals with monetarist theory, and Chapter 7 with civilian budget cuts. Chapter 8 examines broader proposals for restructuring government programs.

Monetarism rests on a nineteenth-century image of the competitive, small-business market economy—and the application of monetarist policy in the 1980s has contained more than a trace of the nineteenth-century version of the trade-off, in which mass unemployment and desperation drove down prices, wages and living standards. The impact of Reaganomics on the labor movement, wages and prices is addressed in Chapter 9.

There are a growing number of proposals for other economic policies for the 1980s. Chapter 10 examines the school of thought known as "neo-liberalism." It focuses on the need to make U.S. industry competitive in world trade, and proposes policies of reindustrialization and retraining aimed at that goal. Chapter 11 looks at another new approach, "economic democracy." It stresses the ways in which our corporate economic system is undemocratic and unsuccessful, and proposes a variety of structural reforms. Some concluding thoughts on the alternatives to Reaganomics are offered in Chapter 12.

chapter 2

does 2+2 equal 7?

Whenever there are great strains or changes in the economic system, it tends to generate crackpot theories, which then find their way into the legislative channels.
—David Stockman

The conservative answer to the problem of stagflation, as to so many other problems, is to use the incentive of higher profits to coax corporations into better behavior. Any limits on private enterprise, whether caused by unions, taxes, government programs or environmental regulations, are simply social debris that must be swept away to clear the broad path to prosperity.

Cruel as it is in human terms, this position has a certain inner logic. Profits are the difference between a firm's selling price and its costs. So to boost profits and hold down prices at the same time, costs must be slashed. Two categories of cost dominate business balance sheets: wages, salaries and fringe benefits absorb two-thirds of all income produced in the corporate sector, and taxes of all types take almost one-sixth. Thus labor costs and corporate taxes, in particular, must be reduced in order to make it profitable to fight inflation.

There are only two ways to cut labor costs: by increasing productivity, the amount a worker produces per hour; or by lowering the amount a worker is paid per hour. Some neo-liberal and economic democracy proposals (see Chapters 10 and 11) emphasize efforts to increase productivity. Conservatives, however, often doubt that much can be done quickly along these lines. In recent years, average output per hour has been stagnant or declining, not rising.

The core of the conservative strategy, therefore, is the fight for lower wages and taxes. Again the arguments are compelling, especially if you are sure, as economists and politicians generally are, that your wages are not the ones being discussed. Lower wages and prices will make U.S. goods more competitive abroad, restoring some of the country's lost international strength. One reason why wages do not fall in recessions is the availability of a wide array of government services and benefits; a rollback of these programs will make workers more insecure, more continuously dependent on employers, more willing to work for less. And some budget cuts will be necessary in any case because the second major plank of the cost-cutting agenda, lower business taxes, will reduce government revenue.

Described in this bald fashion, the conservative answer to stagflation would have limited popular appeal. Blunt advocacy of cuts in wages and social services, combined with tax reductions for business and for the rich, would not win many elections. But, of course, no one campaigns on that basis. The three approaches to economic policy variously employed by the Reagan administration—supply-side economics, military Keynesianism, and monetarism—can be viewed as three marketing strategies, three attempts to get people to support an attack on their own material well-being.

None of the three approaches relies on economic arguments alone. Each embeds its economic policy proposals in a sweeping moral and social vision of Our Way of Life, a call to restore the once and future grandeur of America. The description of each part of Reaganomics, then, must begin with the vision which inspires its supporters.

The wildest and wooliest strand of Reaganomics is certainly supply-side theory. Popular on the campaign trail before the 1980 election, and in Washington in the dreamy months thereafter, supply-side economics has lately fallen somewhat from favor. But it is far from being forgotten. Ronald Reagan remains personally fond of the theory, and continues to push it in policy debates.

The grand vision of the supply-siders can be found in *Wealth and Poverty*, by George Gilder[1]. A best-seller in 1980-81, it is probably the most widely-read book ever produced by the supply-side school. It was described by David Stockman as "Promethean in its intellectual power and insight," and by another Reagan aide as "an inspiration and guide" for the administration. Even Reagan himself is said to have read and liked some shorter articles by Gilder.

So without further ado, welcome to the strange world of George Gilder.

A modest proposal

A state that responds by confiscation and coercion to the inevitable crises....ends by consuming its own people. The rates of taxation climb and the levels of capital decline, until the only remaining wealth beyond the reach of the regime is the very protein of human flesh, and that too is finally taxed, bound, and gagged, and brought to the colossal temple of the state—a final sacrifice of carnal revenue to feed the declining elite.[2]

George Gilder doesn't mince words. Seen through his looking glass, economic planning leads to literal cannibalism. Women earning as much as 80% of male salaries, the situation among blacks today, emasculates the father/provider role, driving men into promiscuous sexuality, drug abuse, and all manner of hedonistic squalor. Italians, Poles and black West Indians in this country all earn more than WASPs do. Contact with God determines which small businesses succeed. The average welfare family has a higher income than the average working family.

Indeed, on reading *Wealth and Poverty* it seems that Gilder is describing a simpler, less crowded planet than the one we live on. Major capitalist enterprises can be ignored because they are, well, boring: "From the point of view of overall economic growth and technological innovation, these leviathans are of little importance to the economy."[3] Accordingly, trade unions, routine or dead-end jobs, fortunes or even comfortably affluent salaries derived from the mainstream of the U.S. economy have all been banished. Gilderland is the scene of more exciting adventures:

The United States is probably the most mobile society in the history of the world. The virtues that are most valuable in it are diligence, discipline, ambition, and a willingness to take risks...Some 400,000 new small businesses are started annually...Business is not only the best route to wealth in America; it is almost the only route for those without education. In business, more-over, the sky is the limit.[4]

The drama of launching new businesses, and the central role they are said to play in the economy, are at times supposed to be a description of reality, at other times an ideal, a faith for which Gilder is crusading. *Wealth and Poverty* is a book which places great stock in the power of positive thinking:

The problem of contemporary capitalism lies not chiefly in a deterioration of physical capital, but in a persistent subversion of the psychological means of production—the morale and inspiration of economic man [sic]...

Or, more tersely (if obscurely), "A capitalist system is chiefly a noosphere, a circuit of ideas and feelings."[5]

A capital idea

If wealth is only an idea in noospheric capitalism, why is it an idea that so few of us have gotten? Gilder's answer appears to be that too many people are living in sin. "Indeed, after work the second principle of upward mobility is the maintenance of monogamous marriage and family." A married man "is spurred by the claims of family to channel his otherwise disruptive male agressions into his performance as a provider for a wife and children."[6] A woman, of course, is supposed to stay home and play Beauty taming the Beast.

The subject of family life is the cue for the entrance by the villains of Gilder's psychodrama: government bureaucrats and feminists. Both profane the sanctity of the male provider role by suggesting that women can get along without men. When a woman receives welfare benefits,

The man has the gradually sinking feeling that his role as provider, the definitive male activity from the primal days of the hunt through the industrial revolution and on into modern life, has been largely seized from him; he has been cuckolded by the compassionate state.

His response to this reality is that very combination of resignation and rage, escapism and violence, short horizons and promiscuous sexuality that characterize everywhere the life of the poor... Boys grow up seeking support from women, while they find manhood in the macho circles of the street and the bar or in the irresponsible fathering of random progeny.[7]

Many liberal and radical critics have noted that Aid to Families with Dependent Children (AFDC) encourages the breakdown of families, since its benefits are much more readily available (in some cases only available) when fathers are absent. Gilder's innovation, aside from nostalgia for the days when women stayed in their place, is his belief that welfare is a comfortable way of life, seducing hard-working people to a life of indolence and marital separation. He insists that the average welfare family of four received close to $18,000 in 1979, somewhat above the median income for the country as a whole. Like many of Gilder's bizarre "facts," this point is documented only by reference to a publication of a right-wing think tank—in this case, *The Welfare Industry*, from the Heritage Foundation.

In reality, AFDC averaged $93 per person per month in 1979.[8] For a four-person family that comes to $4,464 per year. Even with food stamps and Medicaid thrown in, it hardly seems enough to attract many families earning $18,000 a year. And money aside, the well-known degrading treatment of recipients by the welfare system drives most people to find ways off welfare whenever it is economically possible.

Back in Gilderland, however, welfare mothers are living high off the hog. The great fear is that millions more will sign up as soon as they hear the good news. The solution is to slash welfare and Medicaid benefits, to make the dole sufficiently stingy and unpleasant that the idle poor will return to strict male-dominated families, ready to board the big escalator upward.

Climb down from that pole!

The path to prosperity is threatened by more than the largesse of the welfare state. In recent years, feminism has reared its head, demanding that women get equal pay and equal access to jobs. This is unfortunate, because Gilder's men need the money more than women do.

> The man's earnings, unlike the woman's, will determine
> not only his standard of living but also his possibilities
> for marriage and children — whether he can be a sexual
> man. The man's work thus finds its deepest source in
> love.[9]

The disease of equality is more advanced among blacks, where
working women earn 80% as much as men, than among whites,
where the figure is only about 60%. So Gilder's remedy for black
poverty, by which he means black male poverty, is to make black
women poorer.

> Any increase in the independence of black women,
> secured both by welfare and by jobs, will only further
> expand the appalling percentages of black children
> raised without fathers.

Black men don't even benefit much from government anti-
discrimination programs, since they

> are now forced to join an undignified queue with such
> improbable victims as Yale coeds molested by their
> tutors, ex-addicts denied reemployment, assistant pro-
> fessors at Smith rejected for tenure, and telephone oper-
> ators who discover, years later, that what they had
> always wanted was to climb a pole.[10]

Yet even among black men, discrimination isn't really a
problem. Their lower wages, says Gilder, simply result from their
inferior education and skills. (The astute reader will notice that
racism has not entirely vanished from this explanation.) If only
the government would stop carrying on about racism, blacks
would stop being so uppity.

> By cultivating a pervasive expectation of bias and futil-
> ity, a posture of upward resentment and appeals for
> rights rather than upward movement and self-reliance,
> Washington is profoundly damaging the prospects of
> the black poor. At a time when it is hard to find discrim-
> ination anywhere, blacks are being induced to see it
> everywhere....in a world of decreasing bias, the antici-
> pation of it creates an air of ambivalent resignation and

pugnacity unattractive to any employer. Discrimination is not the problem of the American poor.[11]

The answer to poverty couldn't be simpler: quit pretending that discrimination still exists; clamp down on those irresistible welfare checks; and let female earnings sink low enough to rebuild every male ego in sight.

Gilder offers the carrot as well as the stick to the poor. Just keep those families together, keep those male aggressions channeled into economic achievement, and you too can be rich. Follow the example of a Lebanese immigrant family who arrived in Lee, Massachusetts ten years ago, hardly able to speak English. The father got up at five o'clock every morning, drove a hundred miles to a farming area and bought vegetables. The the entire family spent the day selling them at a roadside stand. No time for nonsense like school: "All six children were sources of accumulating capital as they busily bustled around the place." Today that family owns a three-story office building, a few stores, and some nice clothes.[12]

Noticeably lacking from this inspiring tale are any statistics on the percentage of penniless immigrants who own three-story buildings ten years after arrival. For, as even Gilder cannot quite forget, the great majority of small businesses sink rapidly into bankruptcy—often taking their owners' life savings down with them. Since almost everyone fails, why do so many keep trying?

The fact that chance seems to govern success, perhaps a defect in some people's eyes, is to Gilder a great strength.

> Because no one knows which venture will succeed, which number will win the lottery, a society ruled by risk and freedom rather than by rational calculus, a society open to the future rather than planning it, can call forth an endless stream of invention, enterprise and art.

Life as a lottery is the only system compatible with human nature: "The reason capitalism succeeds is that its laws accord with the laws of mind." But by "mind" Gilder does not mean merely one individual.

> The mind has access to a higher consciousness, some-times...called a collective unconscious, sometimes defined as God.

This "awesome contact with cosmic mystery and power" is the hidden force determining who wins the lotteries of life. Ultimately, religious faith

> will lead us to abandon, above all, the idea that the human race can become self-sufficient, can separate itself from chance and fortune in a hubristic siege of rational resource management, income distribution and futuristic planning. Our greatest and only resource is the miracle of human creativity in a relationship of openness to the divine.[13]

The pleasure of giving

If our economy fundamentally consists of God running a gambling casino, then the role of government is that of the casino staff—keeping the gaming tables clean and attractive, and particularly catering to the whims of the biggest spenders. Theology aside, this metaphor undoubtedly captures something about the nature of capitalism. Yet it is not the most flattering image for actual or aspiring capitalists; and Gilder does offer such readers a more palatable self-portrait as well.

In much of the book Gilder relies on the rhetorical equation that investment means giving. He suggests that modern capitalist investment is an updated form of the potlatch custom of the Kwakiutl (native Americans of the Northwest) and other traditional societies, a ceremonial process of feasts and gift-giving provided for the entire tribe by one individual at a time.

> The gifts of advanced capitalism in a monetary economy are called investments...Like gifts, capitalist investments are made without a predetermined return...The gifts will succeed only to the extent that they are altruistic and spring from an understanding of the needs of others.[14]

One might wonder whether employees are also involved in giving, since their efforts on the job necessarily "spring from an understanding of the needs of others." But once again, workers scarcely exist except as potential businessmen of the future. One might also doubt that the Kwakiutl retained legal ownership and control over their gifts after giving them, as capitalists do over investments. The metaphor of giving, though, is a staple feature of Gilder's language. Businesses give, the government takes. Social services can then be described as resting on greed, while investing money is evidence of altruism. Gilder is, of course, free, like Humpty Dumpty in *Through the Looking Glass*, to make words mean whatever he wants them to; the reader is warned that normal usage has been left far behind.

Gilder's economic policy proposals flow directly from the need to prevent bad vibes among the gift-givers, to keep the biggest gamblers coming back to the casino. He is against all manner of controls on business, as conservatives always have been. But aside from the suggestion that economic planning leads to cannibalism—Gilder's forays into anthropology seem to have met with rather limited success—he adds nothing important to the literature of complaints about big government. Where he parts company with traditional conservative thought is in the advocacy of supply-side economics.

Supply-siders argue that past government policy has over-emphasized the "demand side" of the economy. Either by buying things directly, or by giving individuals money to spend, the government helps maintain the demand for goods and services. At the same time, the story goes, increasing taxes (needed to finance all that spending) and regulations have inhibited the "supply side" of the economy, discouraging producers from producing. Thus demand grows faster than supply, and consumers competing for scarce goods and services drive up prices. The solution is to de-emphasize the demand side — cut back government spending—and to stimulate the supply side by reducing the burden of taxes and regulations.

It is one thing to argue that cutting taxes and regulations would have some effect on production and incomes, though possibly a very small effect. Many economists of varying persuasions would agree with that statement. It is another thing, and the mark of the committed supply-siders, to believe that tax cuts and regulatory rollbacks are the necessary and sufficient ingredients to perk up the economy's performance. The debate, in other words, is not about whether supply-side effects exist. It is about whether they are too small to matter or so big that nothing else matters.

George Gilder is not one to support anything halfheartedly. Nothing could be better than a big tax cut when it comes to inspiring investors to give more of their gifts, he says. Taxes are ruining the business world. While the crushing burden of taxation on business investment had escaped the attention of most economists, it "was manifest to a former football player trained in physical education, Congressman Jack Kemp."[15]

Taxes, curves and napkins

Tax cuts are magic. Taxpayers win and the government doesn't lose. That's the message of the Laffer Curve, invented by supply-sider Arthur Laffer, which fascinates Gilder, Jack Kemp and others.

Laffer's argument begins with a question. At what percentage tax rate will the government receive the maximum tax revenue? Imagine that we are talking about the corporate income tax levied on the widget industry. If the government taxes the industry at either 0% or 100% of profits, it will receive no tax revenue. At 0%, the reason is obvious; at 100%, businessmen will lose all incentive to invest in widget-making, and will take their money elsewhere. No widgets will be produced, and no tax will be collected.

At tax rates anywhere between 0% and 100%, however, some widgets will be produced, some profits will be made, and some taxes will be collected. Consider a graph of this relationship, with tax rates from 0% to 100% shown horizontally, and total government revenues from the tax shown vertically, as in Figure 1. (The reader who dislikes graphs may rest assured that the three related graphs in this chapter are the only ones in the book.)

Figure 1

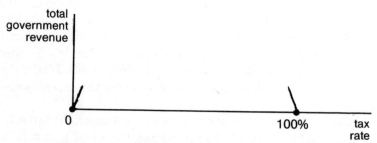

Figure 1: Two little pieces of the Laffer Curve.

There are good reasons to think that the two ends of the graph will look something like the lines shown in Figure 1. If the government raises the tax rate from 0% to, say, 1% or 2% of profits, total tax revenues obviously rise above 0; that's all the left-hand line in Figure 1 is saying. Now suppose the tax rate was formerly 100%, so that no one was producing widgets. If the government then lowers the rate to only 99% or 98%, a few producers may be attracted into the industry. They will presumably pay taxes, so that in this case tax revenues rise as the tax rate is lowered slightly from 100%. That's what the right-hand line in Figure 1 is showing.

With these two pieces of the relationship worked out, and not much else, Arthur Laffer took the fateful next step. Why not assume that the two little lines in Figure 1 are part of a big, smooth curve like the one in Figure 2? Laffer is said to have drawn the complete curve for the first time on a paper napkin at a restaurant.

Figure 2

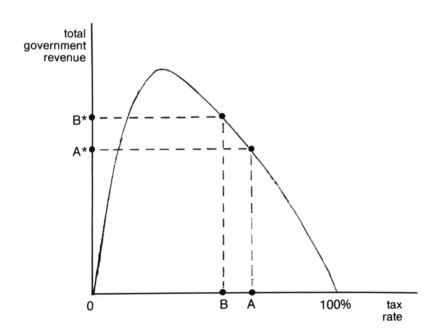

Figure 2: The Laffer Curve, as seen by supply-siders. Cutting the tax rate from A to B would boost government revenue from A* to B*.

The complete Laffer Curve assumes that as the tax rate rises above 0%, total revenues from the tax keep rising up to some maximum. Beyond that point, the added tax burden of higher rates drives down production and profits so fast that government tax revenues actually decrease. The argument for supply-side tax cuts is that, starting from tax rate A in Figure 2, a cut to rate B would produce an increase in revenue from A* to B*.

Not everyone has been blown away by the force of this argument. On a technical level, some economists doubt that there is a simple, smooth curve with a single peak, as drawn in Figure 2, relating tax revenues to tax rates. But even granting the existence of the simple curve, there is a problem which, in a restaurant with larger napkins, Arthur Laffer himself might have noticed.

Crucial to the supply-side argument is the claim that the present tax rate, like point A in Figure 2, is to the right of the peak of the Laffer Curve. In that case, a cut of the correct size could raise tax revenues. But what if the current tax rate is to the left of the peak, like C in Figure 3? In that case, a cut in taxes, for instance to rate D, produces a drop in tax revenues from C* to D*.

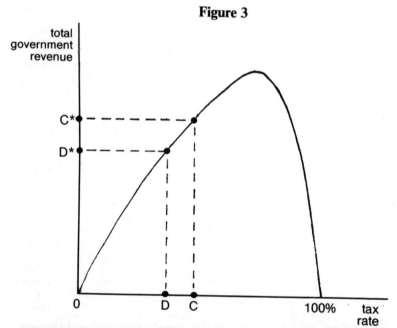

Figure 3

Figure 3: The Laffer Curve, as seen by everyone else. If the current tax rate C is to the left of the peak of the graph, a cut to tax rate D lowers revenue from C* to D*.

So the key question is, which side of the peak of the curve are we on? The entire supply-side case rests on the unproved assertion that we are on the right-hand side, as drawn in Figure 2, that tax rates are so high that business is flattened, exertion and innovation squelched, etc., etc.

For a devout supply-sider like George Gilder, the destructive impact of taxes is simply an article of faith. Why bother investing if the profits will all be taxed away? It's more fun to relax and go sailing instead of doing all that hard, creative work of giving gifts to the economy.

This, then, is the supply-side credo: tax cuts mean workers will work more; investors will invest more; production will rise. Inflation will be cured by increased production, since when there's more of something its price drops. Even government budget deficits will go down, not up, due to the magic of (the right-hand side of) the Laffer Curve. If supply-siders were arithmetic teachers, we might well learn that 2+2 now equals 7. But alas for Gilder and his ilk, there is considerable evidence, discussed in the next chapter, that the real world doesn't live up to the supply-side dreams.

Myths and policies

The more that people understand it, the less popular the right-wing economic program is likely to be. The "Robin Hood in reverse" flavor of taking from the poor to give to the rich and to the military is no coincidence, no regrettable necessity forced on us by the logic of fiscal responsibility. It is essential to the conservative strategy of fighting inflation by boosting profits and holding down wages and business taxes.

There are some things that can't be talked about in plain English, however. Ideologues like George Gilder play the vital role of making the destruction of social welfare programs look attractive to the people who benefit from them, of preparing a broad consensus for policies that will weaken the economic position of most working people. It is done with myths about the merits of capitalism, and with policies that purport to solve the economy's problems.

Gilder's myth is a sweeping, inspirational-sounding one. You are potentially one of the most important businessmen in the economy (or his wife, as the case may be). Investment is giving, the creative, altruistic act that makes things go. You too can do it!

All it takes is hard work, patriarchal and monogamous families, willingness to gamble against ridiculous odds, refusal to listen to claptrap about government benefits, and mystical belief in a profoundly irrational deity. Gilder's unique accomplishment, aside from reminding us of the threat of cannibalism, is to blend several apparently disparate elements of New Right politics: anti-feminism, fundamentalist religion, and supply-side economics are revealed to be intimately connected, at least in one writer's view.

When it comes to policy, Gilder advocates another one of those daring gambles. How much will you bet that a giant tax cut for the rich is the route to renewed growth and prosperity? It can be thought of as a social science experiment, a laboratory test which only the occupant of the Oval Office can perform. To find out if the supply-siders are right, just talk Congress into an immense tax cut, and then watch to see if tax revenues go up or down. If they go up, your popularity and your place in history will be assured. And if somehow they go down, if the federal deficit heads toward $200 billion a year, well, nobody's perfect. . .

chapter 3

for the taxpayer who has everything

Unlike some past tax "reforms," this is not merely a shift of wealth between different sets of taxpayers. This proposal for an equal reduction in everyone's tax rates will expand our national prosperity, enlarge national incomes, and increase opportunities for all Americans.
—Ronald Reagan, 1981

The president was wrong on the two most important points about his tax cut. First, it was a shift of wealth between different groups, giving more to those who already had the most. Three hidden biases made this "equal reduction in everyone's tax rates" nearly worthless to those on the bottom, but invaluable to those on top.

And second, the tax cut did not expand prosperity, enlarge incomes, or increase opportunities for most people. A variety of evidence, ranging from academic studies to the obvious experience of the early 1980s, shows that massive tax cuts do very little to increase the supply of labor, savings or investment.

Bias #1: Some are more equal than others

One of Reagan's most popular campaign promises in 1980 was the 30% across-the-board tax cut. Scaled down to 23% but otherwise largely unchanged, it was passed by Congress in August 1981. Most people, failing to understand the intricacies of

33

the income tax system, thought this meant everyone would pay 30%, or later 23%, less in income taxes. Even if that were the case (which it is not), the tax cut would still favor the rich.

How could cutting everyone's taxes by the same percentage favor one group over another? A numerical example may help clarify the issue. Consider the effects of a 23% reduction in income taxes on two hypothetical families, as shown in Table 1. The rich family has a $60,000 income, of which $18,000 is paid in income taxes; the average family has a $20,000 income, on which it pays $2,000 in taxes. (These are approximately the taxes paid by a family of four taking the standard deduction in 1980.)

Table 1: Effects of an Across-the-Board Tax Cut		
	Rich family	**Average family**
1. Income before tax	$60,000	$20,000
2. Tax	18,000	2,000
3. Income after tax	42,000	18,000
4. Tax cut (23% of line 2)	4,140	460
5. Relative gain from tax cut (line 4 as % of line 3)	9.9%	2.6%

A 23% tax cut is worth $4,140 to the rich family, a gain of almost 10% in their after-tax income. For the average family, 23% of their taxes is only $460, less than 3% of their after-tax income. An across-the-board cut is tilted toward the rich because the income tax is a "progressive" tax: the higher your income, the greater the percentage it takes. In Table 1, the rich family was paying 30% of its income before the cut, while the average family was paying only 10%. So the tax cut gave the rich family 23% of 30% of its before-tax income, while it gave the average family only 23% of 10% of its income.

This sort of bias is not an inevitable feature of all income tax cuts. It would be easy to cut tax rates more sharply for lower-income groups. It would be equally possible to cut other taxes which fall most heavily on low- and middle-income taxpayers. The Social Security tax, for instance, takes a bigger bite out of many people's paychecks than does the income tax. Social Security takes a constant percentage out of your wages, salary or self-employment income, up to a ceiling ($35,200 in 1983, likely about $39,000 in 1984). It takes nothing from other forms of income, such as interest or dividends, and it takes nothing from the part of your earnings (if any) above the ceiling.

In other words, Social Security is a "regressive" tax: people below the ceiling pay a higher percentage of their incomes in Social Security taxes than people above it. An across-the-board cut in Social Security taxes would therefore return a greater percentage of income to people below the ceiling. This alternative seems to have escaped the notice of the White House tax-cutters; instead, Social Security taxes have been increased. On the other hand, estate and gift taxes, paid almost exclusively by the rich, have been all but abolished under Reagan.

Bias #2: Bracket creep, high and low

Biased as an across-the-board cut in income taxes would have been, the tax cut adopted in 1981 was even worse. The principal reason is that this tax cut, unlike most previous ones, failed to increase the size of the personal exemptions or standard deduction. This will be easier to understand after a quick review of the nuts and bolts of the income tax system.

The IRS allows you to exempt $1,000 of income for yourself, plus another $1,000 for each dependent, from any income tax. Then, if you do not itemize deductions, the next chunk of income—the standard deduction, or, in IRS newspeak, the "zero bracket amount"—is also yours to keep. For a married couple filing jointly, the standard deduction is $3,400; for a single individual, it is $2,300.

After that, unless you qualify for any of the more esoteric exemptions and exclusions, you begin paying the IRS. In 1980, before the Reagan cuts, a married couple paid 14% of the first $2,100 above exemptions and deductions, 16% of the next $2,100, 18% of the next $4,300, and so on. As income rose the tax rate increased through fifteen steps, or tax brackets, finally peaking at a top rate of 70% on income above $212,000. For a single taxpayer the brackets start at lower points; 1980's top rate of 70% was paid on income above $106,000.

As you move into higher brackets, you don't pay the higher rate on your whole income—only on the part which falls into each bracket. A family with $250,000 income would have been described as being "in the 70% bracket" in 1980, but still got the regular exemptions and deductions, paid only 14% on their next $2,100, and so on through all the brackets. Only on the part of their income, after deductions and exemptions, that exceeded $212,000 did they pay 70%.

The system of exemptions, deductions and rising rates in higher brackets makes the income tax quite progressive. Loopholes aside, it is structured to take a larger percentage out of big incomes than out of small ones. But that same structure has a perverse effect in times of inflation. If your before-tax income rises just fast enough to keep up with inflation, your taxes will go up even faster as more of your income is pushed into higher brackets. Known as "bracket creep," the phenomenon is quite important: at 1980 tax rates, every 10% increase in income produced a 15% to 16% increase in income taxes.

At first glance, the Reagan tax cut looks like the answer to bracket creep. After all, the rates in each bracket were reduced by 23%. But the tax cut did nothing about the form of bracket creep most serious for those on the bottom. For lower-income people the rates in each bracket are less important than the size of the exemptions and deductions. The failure to increase exemptions and deductions in a time of inflation means that a decreasing fraction of your income is free from tax. For the poor, the result is a tax increase.

Imagine a two-parent family of four who received $10,000 in 1980. They got four personal exemptions of $1,000 each, and the standard deduction of $3,400, for a total of $7,400 of tax-free income. Only $2,600, about a quarter of their income, was subject to tax.

Now suppose that prices rise 30% from 1980 to 1984. If the family has exactly kept up with inflation, their 1984 income is $13,000. But they still get only $7,400 tax-free. They now have $5,600, or more than two-fifths of their income, subject to tax.

The result is that despite the tax cut, their taxes rise much faster than inflation. In 1980 they paid $374, or 3.7% of their income; in 1984 they pay $679, or 5.2% of their income. Bracket creep is alive and well at the lower end of the income distribution.

The failure to increase exemptions and deductions affects everyone, not just the poor. But at higher income levels it is of smaller relative importance, and is balanced or outweighed by the cuts in tax rates. Table 2 shows the changing tax burden at different income levels, using the same assumption—family income just keeping up with 30% inflation from 1980 to 1984—at each level.

For a family with $20,000 in 1980, there is a slight reduction in income tax burden, from 11.3% to 11.1%, but it is swamped by the Social Security tax increase. Even for the family with $35,000 in 1980, the total tax burden increases by 1984. And five-sixths of all U.S. households made less than $35,000 in 1980.[1] The people whose tax burden was lowered by Reagan's policies, shown toward the bottom of table 2, are very special people indeed.

Table 2: The Federal Tax Burden Before and After the Reagan Cuts				
	Income tax as a percentage of family income		Income and Social Security taxes as a percentage of family income	
Family income 1980	1980	1984	1980	1984
$ 10,000	3.7%	5.2%	9.9%	12.2%
20,000	11.3	11.1	17.5	18.1
35,000	18.9	18.4	25.0	25.4
50,000	24.2	22.1	30.4	29.1
100,000	35.7	30.8	38.9	35.0
250,000	49.5	39.2	50.8	40.9

Notes: Each family's income is assumed to rise 30% from 1980 to 1984, equal to the estimated rate of inflation. All income taxes are for a married couple filing jointly with four personal exemptions. Those at the lowest three income levels are assumed to take the standard deduction in both years. All others are assumed to claim itemized deductions equal to 10% of their incomes in both years (the level of deductions assumed by the Census Bureau in similar tables).

At the lowest four income levels, all income is assumed subject to Social Security tax; for the $35,000-$50,000 families, this implies that there are two salary earners in the family, and no sources of income other than salaries. For the highest two income levels in the table, the family is assumed to have two salary earners each paying the maximum Social Security tax.

Assuming a lower rate of inflation would reduce the 1984 tax burden slightly at all levels, but would not change the general conclusion that the rich gain the most. At 27% inflation over the four-year period, the family with $35,000 in 1980 would "break even," showing the same 25.0% total tax burden in both years. Thus the five-sixths of the population with lower incomes would still have an increased tax burden.

Sources: IRS, *Form 1040 General Instructions, 1980*, ScheduleY; *Economic Recovery Tax Act of 1981*, U.S. House of Representatives Report 97-215, p. 6; *New York Times*, 11/9/82 and 3/10/83 (on Social Security).

Bias #3: A Trojan Horse

The higher your income, as shown in Table 2, the juicier the fruits of the Reagan tax cut. This may have been the point all along. As David Stockman said about the Kemp-Roth bill, the original proposal on which the 1981 tax cut was based,

> The hard part of the supply-side tax cut is dropping the top rate from 70 to 50 percent—the rest of it is a secondary matter. The original argument was that the top bracket was too high. And that's having the most devastating effect on the economy. Then, the general argument was that, in order to make this palatable as a political matter, you had to bring down all the brackets. But, I mean, Kemp-Roth was always a Trojan horse to bring down the top rate.

The third bias of the tax cut is the most brazen. Despite repeated presidential statements that all tax rates were being cut equally, it was simply not true. The people at the very top got their rates cut farther and faster than the rest of us.

Two different rules appear to have been used in making up the reductions in tax rates. Rule number one, the widely advertised procedure, was that the tax rates in most brackets were to be reduced in three steps—in October 1981, July 1982, and July 1983—for a total reduction of 23%. But at upper income levels this was superceded by rule number two, the hidden contents of Stockman's Trojan horse: all rates above 50% were to be cut to 50%, effective immediately.

Rule number two had no effect on the first 11 of the 15 tax brackets, covering your family's first first $85,600. In brackets 12 and 13, applying to your income between $85,600 and $162,400, rule number two meant that you got your whole 23% tax cut at once in late 1981, while the peasants had to wait two more years for theirs. And in brackets 14 and 15, covering only income beyond your family's first $162,400, the tax rates were cut by 26% and 29%, respectively, all in 1981. This, combined with the other biases, accounts for the immense generosity of the Reagan tax cut for those at the very top. As shown in Table 2, a family receiving $250,000 in 1980 knocked ten percentage points off its tax burden in just four years.

To summarize, the 1981 cut in personal income taxes was inequitable in three ways. First, even if it had been, as was widely believed, an equal percentage reduction in everyone's income tax, it would still have given a greater percentage increase in after-tax income to the rich. Second, the failure to raise the personal exemption and standard deduction resulted in a tax increase for many poor people. Finally, despite all the rhetoric of equality, the changes in tax rates were explicitly tilted in favor of the very rich.

After 1984 a different kind of change is scheduled to take place, known as "indexing." The rates in each tax bracket will remain fixed, but the income levels at which the brackets begin will be indexed to inflation—that is, increased each year at the same rate as inflation. At that time the personal exemption and standard deduction will be indexed to inflation as well. This will prevent the income tax structure from becoming any more tilted toward the rich, and will finally eliminate bracket creep.

Raising the exemptions, deductions and brackets along with inflation will tend to freeze the relative distribution of the tax burden at the point it reached in 1984. And at that point, the income tax weighs much more heavily on the poor, and more lightly on the rich, than it did in 1980.

Bitter medicine, or just bitter?

The biases of the tax cut are a sufficient rebuttal to the alleged populism of Reaganomics. There is no basis for the notion that everyone has benefitted equally. But this does not deal with the second major point, the dramatic supply-side effects said to result from tax cuts.

Lower tax rates are supposed to increase the supply of labor and capital by inspiring us all to work more, save more and invest more. Productivity, profits, growth and employment then will soar; eventually the deserts will bloom. Inequity in the short run might then be an unavoidable side effect of a policy that will get the economy growing again, to everyone's long-run benefit. In the words of John F. Kennedy, frequently quoted by supply-side economists today, "A rising tide lifts all boats."

The sad truth, however, is that the evidence overwhelmingly disagrees with the supply-siders.[2] Clearly the supply-side policies initiated in 1981 did not lead to any surge of growth; if anything the economy surged downward, closer to a depression than at any time since the 1930s. Academic studies of the response to tax incentives, too, confirm the negative conclusion. There are three main areas in which tax cuts are alleged to stimulate the economy: in increasing the amount of work, the amount of savings, and the amount of investment being done. In each case the supply-siders have very little ground to stand on.

In the textbook fable of economics, the amount of work that is done depends on workers' individual choices between labor and leisure. The "price" of an hour of leisure is the income given up by not working for that hour—in other words, the take-home pay for an additional hour of work. The higher the price of leisure becomes, the more workers will choose labor rather than leisure, and work additional hours. So cuts in tax rates, by raising take-home pay, will induce people to put in more time at work. Implausible as it may sound, this really is the supply-side theory about how to boost the supply of labor.

Even in the realm of textbook economics there is a problem with this argument. There are two conflicting effects of an increase in hourly take-home pay. On the one hand, some people will be inspired to work more, willing to give up another hour at the beach for $8 but not for $6. On the other hand, some people will find that they can now make enough to live on with fewer hours of work and choose to spend more time at the beach. (Textbooks call these the "substitution effect" and the "income effect" respectively.) There is no way to determine in the abstract which effect will be larger.

In the real world almost no one is invited to decide exactly how many hours to work, let alone being free to change that decision every time tax rates are altered. Industrial jobs that involve overtime typically give workers little or no choice about how much overtime to work. Most other jobs have hours rigidly fixed in advance. The world of free-lancers, consultants, shop-keepers and other self-employed people who control their own hours is a small part of the labor force.

The only way to make sense of the textbook fable is to interpret it as describing choices about the number of jobs being done. Some people can postpone retirement, work second jobs or switch from part-time to full-time employment. Most important, some families can increase the number of family members working outside the home.

Yet there is less room left for increasing the number of workers than there used to be. More than 90% of men between the ages of 20 and 55 are in the labor force (either holding or actively seeking paid employment); many of the others are enrolled in higher education, sick or disabled. In the same age range, more than 60% of women are in the labor force. While there can be some further increase, the lack of adequate child care (a worsening problem thanks to recent budget cuts) makes it unlikely that both women and men can work outside the home at the rates that men do today.

Moreover, it is not clear why it is even desirable to increase the number of people trying to work right now. There are millions of people already looking for work but unable to find it. The grand sweep of supply-side theory tends to brush such pedestrian details out of sight.

Many economists have done statistical studies of the effect of after-tax wages on the amount of work people do. Most studies agree that for men, a wage increase leads to a slight decrease in hours worked. In the textbook terms, the income effect is slightly greater than the substitution effect. Estimates of the effect of a 1% wage hike on men range from no change to a 0.4% decrease in hours worked.

Among women higher wages inspire more work; a 1% wage hike may produce a 0.8% or 0.9% increase in hours worked by women, though estimates as low as a 0.1% decrease and as high as a 2.0% increase have been published. Combining the results for men and women, a recent review of the economic literature concluded that a 1% wage increase probably would prompt a 0.15% increase in total hours of work.[3]

So suppose that in 1980 there had been no serious unemployment, so that anyone who wanted to could have gotten a job. And suppose that there had been no problems of inflation and bracket creep eroding the value of a tax cut, and that everyone's taxes actually had been reduced by 23%. (These assumptions, of course, are all more favorable to the supply-side argument than the real world has been.) For the average family in 1980, a 23% reduction in taxes would have meant a 7% increase in take-home pay for any additional hours of work.

Using the combined male/female estimate from the economic literature, a 7% pay increase would lead to a 1% increase in hours worked. (That is, 7 times 0.15% is about 1%.) Under ideal conditions, in other words, Reagan's tax cut might have increased the supply of labor by 1%. In the real world, where high unemployment and bracket creep interfere with even this modest supply-side effect, the impact of a 23% tax cut on the supply of labor may for all practical purposes be ignored.

A billion saved is a billion earned

Supply-side theory does not pin all its hopes on increases in the supply of labor. Tax cuts are also supposed to boost savings, thereby increasing the funds that businesses can borrow for expansion. While most of us are agonizing over the choice between labor and leisure, the rich are debating the merits of saving for the future vs. immediate consumption. (In the textbooks, everyone makes this choice, too; but in reality only the rich have significant-sized savings.) The theory of the two choices is exactly parallel: the "price" of consuming now is the interest foregone by not saving the money. A tax cut gives savers a higher after-tax interest rate, helping to tip the balance toward saving.

One theoretical problem with this analysis is, again, the clash between the substitution effect and the income effect. Higher after-tax interest rates will inspire some wealthy individuals to save more, while others will reach their desired level of interest income with less savings than before, and spend more on caviar instead of bonds. Studies of the effect of changing interest rates on savings have yielded ambiguous and inconclusive results; most economists do not believe there is any proven effect. A controversial 1978 study, often cited by supply-siders, claimed to find a big effect of interest rates on savings. But other economists have found many flaws in the study, and its result is not widely accepted.[4]

The importance of providing incentives to savers, however, was firmly embedded in the 1981 tax cut. The rich receive not only the benefit of the tilt in the new tax rates as described above; they also get several specific new loopholes for certain types of savings.

You can now put up to $2,000 a year into a tax-free Individual Retirement Account (IRA). No money can be withdrawn from an IRA, without paying a stiff penalty, until you reach age 59½. You pay no taxes on the amounts you put in, and on the interest received, until you withdraw it — at which time you will likely have a lower income, and hence fall into a lower tax bracket, than in your working years.

Another new loophole was the misnamed "All-Savers" program, announced with great fanfare in late 1981. Special one-year savings bonds were issued, on which the first $1,000 interest per person was tax-free. The catch was that the interest rate on these bonds was well below the market rate, making them worthwhile only if you were in a high tax bracket. People below $30,000 - $40,000 in income, in other words most people, did better putting whatever savings they had into higher-interest, taxable alternatives such as money market funds.

Yet another egalitarian loophole now allows everyone, rich and poor alike, to receive $750 of public utility company dividends tax-free so long as the money is reinvested in the utility's stocks. Such a specific pork-barrel provision does undoubtedly encourage reinvestment in the utility industry. But that is a far cry from concluding that savings throughout the economy have been increased. The utilities' gain might be coming at the expense of lower reinvestment in other industries.

The same question can be raised about all the incentives: are they adding to savings or just taking money out of one form of savings and putting it into another? In 1982 an immense $35 billion was deposited in IRAs. But, according to analyses by both the Treasury Department and Merrill Lynch, Pierce, Fenner & Smith, little or none of this was new savings. Most of it was simply transferred out of existing, often taxable, savings accounts. There was no noticeable increase in the overall rate of savings.[5]

However, all those transfers of funds into IRAs lowered a lot of people's tax bills. And when people pay less in taxes, the deficit increases. The Treasury analysis found that the tax break for IRAs increased the 1982 deficit by about $5 billion. When the deficit increases, the government borrows more, competing with private business for whatever funds are available. In this case, the government had to borrow $5 billion more because of IRAs.

This leads to one of the ultimate ironies of supply-side incentives. Tax loopholes for savers, like the IRA, are justified by the claim that they will make more savings available for business; in fact, they probably leave less for the private sector. The first year of IRAs increased government demand for funds by $5 billion, while causing little or no increase in the supply of funds. On balance, business was left with almost $5 billion less for investment. (An involved set of calculations shows that the same general conclusion normally holds for tax incentives for savers: the deficit, and government borrowing, will increase faster than the supply of private savings.[6])

With their array of loopholes for savings, the supply-siders achieved just the opposite of their announced intentions. While putting additional billions into some already stuffed pockets, they likely made less, not more, money available for businesses to borrow and invest.

Corporate taxes: an endangered species

Even if the savings incentives somehow were to work, they would be of little relevance to the actual process of business investment. Savings by individuals have always been a relatively minor source of corporate funds. In 1979, for instance, personal savings were $86 billion, while corporations' own funds available for investment (profits remaining after dividend payments and taxes, plus depreciation allowances) totalled $313 billion. More-over, $79 billion was invested in housing in 1979, almost equal to the volume of personal savings. Textbook mythology asserts that individual household decisions about savings provide the funds for business investment; it would be closer to the truth to say that household savings finance housing, and corporate funds finance corporate investment.

The supply-siders did not forget the corporations at tax-cutting time in 1981. To begin with, various tidbits were tossed into some of the usual hungry mounths. New exemptions from the windfall oil profits tax, to cite just one example, will be worth over $3 billion annually by 1986. On the subject of the new loopholes for particular corporate interests, it is hard to be more emphatic than David Stockman.

> Do you realize the greed that came to the forefront? The hogs were really feeding. The greed level, the level of opportunism, just got out of control.

The main course offered to the business world, though, was much bigger than any of the specific loopholes like the windfall profits exemption. Known in the jargon of official Washington as "capital cost recovery provisions," the principal 1981 corporate tax cut was estimated to cost the Treasury $53 billion a year by 1986, and far more in later years. About half of this was repealed in 1982 (the only area discussed so far which was significantly affected by the 1982 tax bill), but business was still left with half of the largest tax cut anyone had dreamed possible. The most important parts of the business tax cut were changes in the tax treatment of depreciation and increases in the investment tax credit—matters which require another brief detour through the workings of the tax laws before they can be explained.

Imagine for a moment that you are a businessman trying to avoid paying taxes. The corporate income tax takes a percentage of your profits, which are the difference between your sales revenues and your costs. The more you pad your costs, the lower your reported profits, and your taxes, will be. Depreciation is one of the easiest costs to pad.

Suppose you have just bought a machine which will wear out in ten years. You need to save one-tenth of the cost of the machine each year, so that you can afford to replace it in ten years. This is a genuine cost of doing business, and it is the idea behind depreciation allowances. The IRS allows you to call that amount of savings a (tax-free) cost, rather than a (taxable) part of profits.

But the lifetime of a machine is often hard to predict in advance. The shorter you can claim the machine's lifetime will be, the sooner you can set aside the cost of the machine into your tax-free depreciation allowance. Getting the money exempted from tax sooner rather than later can be worth quite a lot to you in times of high interest rates.

IRS rules governing the rate at which depreciation allowances can be taken have long been the focus of intense business lobbying. While these rules have become steadily more generous to corporate taxpayers, all past tax laws preserved at least some attempt at determining the actual productive life of business assets, and tied depreciation schedules to those lifetimes. In 1981 the corporate community and its elected representatives had a better idea. Why not pick some very short lifetimes and arbitrarily apply them to all assets?

The result is a system that allows faster depreciation than anyone would have dared to ask for just a few years ago. There are now four categories of property. Cars, trucks, research equipment, older racehorses and other short-lived apparatus can be depreciated over three years. Most other machinery and equipment, younger racehorses, farm buildings and petroleum storage facilities are considered to last five years. Most other buildings and railroad cars are assigned a ten-year lifetime, except for most public utility property, which is assumed to endure for all of fifteen years. (Under the previous law, some equipment had a tax lifetime as long as 36 years, and some buildings had to be depreciated over a 60-year period.) In almost every case, the new figures are ludicrously shorter than the expected useful life of the assets involved. Thus the tax-free depreciation allowances can be built up long before the buildings and equipment physically wear out, amounting to a big tax break.

An additional sweetener sprinkled on top was the increase in the investment tax credit. This credit lets businesses deduct from their taxes a percentage of the price of most new investments. The new rates—a 6% credit for assets in the three-year depreciation category, and 10% in all other categories, are an increase for most assets. (However, the 1982 tax hike lowered slightly the amount of depreciation that could be claimed on any property which had also received an investment tax credit.)

The combination of investment tax credits and fast depreciation works wonders in reducing a company's tax bill. But it does nothing for businesses that are already paying no taxes, either because they are losing money or because they qualify for more than enough loopholes. The 1981 tax cut set out to address this glaring inequity by introducing a brand new scam, allowing companies to buy and sell tax breaks by pretending to lease equipment to each other.

As the size and scope of this tax dodge became apparent, however, a minor flurry of protest arose. Even some business leaders were heard to worry about the threat of a public backlash if corporations appeared to be grabbing too much all at once. We wouldn't want to kill the goose that had just laid so many golden eggs, would we? The opportunity to transfer tax breaks through phony leasing arrangements was abolished in 1982, with only token protests from business.

The corporate income tax had already been shrinking before the Reagan administration. From 29% of all federal revenue in 1955, it had withered away to 15% in 1979. Further shrinkage is clearly in store: after the 1981 cuts, corporate taxes were predicted to become extinct by 1990; with the 1982 amendments, business income taxes may not quite vanish, but will become an endangered species.

If high taxes have been choking off business investment, as the supply-side enthusiasts believe, then it would be hard to imagine anything better than the 1981 tax cut for perking up the economy. Yet here, as with savings incentives, economic studies do not show convincing evidence for the influence of tax rates on investment decisions. Several recent surveys of economic research have concluded that tax rates and other factors affecting the availability and cost of funds are all less important than demand in determining investment. In plain English, the studies seem to show that businesses are willing to invest when they see growing markets for their products, and reluctant to spend money, regardless of tax incentives, when they don't see those markets.

In real life, the business world appears to agree more with the results of these studies than with the hopes of the supply-siders. Following the adoption of the tax cut, the economy sank into recession, due in part to a drop in business investment. As *Business Week* observed in November 1981, events were more in line with the views of John Maynard Keynes, the original "demand-side" theorist.

> The investment slump has to be deeply disturbing to the Administration's supply-side theorists. In their view of the world, business should already be responding to the new incentives provided by the tax cuts retroactive to the beginning of the year. Instead, companies seem to be acting on a Keynesian premise that investment plans respond mainly to a surge in demand that pushes up operating rates. It is still too early to give a final grade to the supply-side view of the investment process. But it is clear that the theory has flunked the mid-term.[7]

While the tax cut has produced no measurable increase in spending on new physical assets, it has given the business world more money to play with. A new wave of merger mania has swept the country, as corporations "invest" in attempts to buy each other's stock. The steel industry, for example, badly in need of modernization, is said to be spending less than $4 billion a year on its plants and equipment. Yet U.S. Steel was able to celebrate the first anniversary of Reagan's inauguration by spending more than $6 billion to acquire Marathon Oil. Such speculative pursuits will be all that the business tax cut inspires, as long as the prospects for new productive investment remain bleak.

What next?

In short, supply-side tax cuts are as ineffective as they are inequitable. They do not produce noticeable increases in the supply of labor, savings or investment. They simply produce a steep tilt of the tax system toward those who already had the most.

The failure of supply-side incentives is no longer exactly news. In the absence of the promised surge in production and incomes, the big tax cut has simply led to a big deficit — to the embarrassment of conservative Republicans who have always made a shibboleth of balanced budgets.

To the hard-core supply-siders, the problem is that taxes were not cut fast enough. Perhaps if we had had the whole 23% tax cut in the first year, the deserts would be blooming after all. More pragmatic policymakers, faced with inescapable evidence that they were, indeed, flunking the midterm, scrambled to catch up before the final. Some searched for ever-deeper budget cuts— but the sheer size of the 1981 tax breaks, hundreds of billions of dollars a year by the late 1980s, dwarfs the results of David Stockman's penny-pinching orgies. Others advocated "revenue enhancements," or, as they are known outside the nation's capital, tax increases.

The 1982 tax hike represented a triumph of the pragmatists over the supply-siders. Yet aside from repealing a chunk of the business tax cut, it undid very little of the damage done in 1981. As originally proposed, it was no more than one-quarter the size of the total 1981 cut—and it soon became even smaller. Originally the 1982 law included some levies falling most heavily on the poor, such as increased cigarette and telephone taxes, and some on the rich, primarily the withholding requirement for interest and dividends. A massive lobbying campaign by the banking industry, however, defeated the idea that coupon-clippers should be subject to the same withholding rules as mere wage-earners. And with that gone, the surviving 1982 tax increases on individuals fell most heavily on the poor.

Supply-side theory may now be largely discredited; it may no longer be the terms in which policies are framed and defended. But the wreckage the supply-siders made of the federal tax system has not been repaired. The gaping deficits of the Reagan years reflect above all the generosity shown to business and to the rich in the early 1980s.

chapter 4

the
smell
of
success

*Avoiding defects is not costless. Those who have low
aversion to risk—relative to money—will be most likely
to purchase cheap, unreliable products. Agency action
to impose quality standards interferes with the efficient
expression of consumer preferences.*

> —from a 1980 report co-authored by James
> C. Miller III, later appointed by Reagan to
> head the Federal Trade Commission

Unfettered free enterprise is all the rage in Ronald Reagan's
Washington. But hearing that the head of the FTC had advocated
the freedom to sell junk to poor people was an embarrassment
even to the administration's friends in business. "It's crazy," said
a U.S. Chamber of Commerce executive. "Industry is not in favor
of making defective products—think of the product liability
suits—and it has no intention of doing so."[1]

Industry definitely is in favor, however, of the bulk of
Reagan's program of deregulation. Conservatives of all stripes
have long groused about government interference; supply-siders
turned this complaint into a foundation of their theory. The idea
is that deregulation, like tax cuts, should free business to expand
its profits, production and employment. Yet reality has once
again eluded the supply-siders' grasp. Deregulation does not
prompt a surge of prosperity; in some cases, corporations
actually do better when the government regulates them.

The deregulatory crusade employs a favorite technique of economists, known as cost-benefit analysis. The costs to business of complying with a regulation are supposed to be weighed against the benefits to society. If the costs are greater, the regulation gets canned.

Many of the benefits of regulation are hard to measure in dollars: what value should be placed on avoiding illnesses, injuries and deaths? Economists have tried, nonetheless, to estimate the monetary worth of such benefits, often by counting insurance premiums, medical expenses and lost wages as the cost of illness or injury.

It should be noted that this approach is far from satisfactory. The "cost" of an injury in lost wages is greatest if it happens to a white male, for instance. Moreover, the economists' estimates completely fail to capture the non-financial, human impact of disability or death. Thus there is a persistent tendency toward understating benefits—as can be seen in one example of cost-benefit analysis.

Writing in the wake of the 1982 Tylenol poisonings, Yale University economist Paul MacAvoy seriously argued that the government should not require tamper-proof packaging on over-the-counter drugs. The benefit, according to MacAvoy, was the value of saving your life, which he priced at a million dollars, multiplied by the risk that your package of Tylenol has been poisoned, which he estimated at one chance in one hundred million. In other words, the benefit was about one penny per package. Yet tamper-proof seals might cost two to ten cents per package. To MacAvoy it was clear that the cost far exceeds the benefit, so tamper-proof packaging should not be required.[2]

(Johnson & Johnson, the makers of Tylenol, strangely chose to ignore MacAvoy's advice. Without even waiting for government regulation, they quickly began a very successful advertising campaign, which stressed that all new Tylenol packages were tamper-proof.)

When an established economist spends his time denouncing tamper-proof pill bottles, it may seem merely funny. But the broader assault on regulations is deadly serious. While regulatory bodies throughout the federal government are under fire, the attack has been concentrated on a handful of newer agencies, such as the Occupational Health and Safety Administration (OSHA) and the Environmental Protection Agency (EPA), and on the Interior Department's restrictions on private use of federal lands.

The most remarkable fact about these regulations is that by many standards they have been successful. And in areas such as toxic waste disposal or the massive pollution created by the energy industry, there is unmistakable evidence that more, not less, regulation is needed.

This is not to say that all government rules are sensible or worth preserving. But the occasional attack on obviously silly rules is only the loss-leader of the deregulatory sales pitch, a throwaway designed to attract popular support. In a press conference on November 10, 1981, for example, Reagan described the case of Katie Beckett, a partially paralyzed three-year-old who had been in a hospital since the age of four months. Although Katie could receive better and cheaper care at home, Social Security's Supplemental Security Income program would only pay her medical bills if she remained hospitalized.

On November 12, SSI rules were waived to allow Katie to return home without loss of benefits, making Katie and her parents much happier as well as saving the government money. But this was only a one-time propaganda ploy. Two months later, when asked whether there had been other waivers of the rules in similar cases, a Social Security official said, "That decision applied to her only, and there have been no other exceptions made."[3]

Katie's story scored a rhetorical point for the Reagan administration. But it is not for the sake of other people like her that regulations have been rolled back.

Count it again, Murray

Most regulations are by no means as silly as the one which kept Katie Beckett in a hospital. In general, at least four kinds of evidence confirm the success of environmental and safety regulations. First, even the administration's style of cost-benefit analysis, done correctly, shows that many regulations are worthwhile. Second, the much-touted paperwork burden created by regulations turns out to be quite small. Third, many businesses have developed new lines of profitable production in response to regulations. Finally, there is direct evidence of declining levels of pollution in the years since environmental regulation began.

While denunciation of occasional silly rules may create the impression that there are no real benefits of regulation, a new brand of statistics-mongering suggests that there are immense costs. Murray Weidenbaum, chairman of the Council of Economic Advisors in 1981-82, specializes in writing about the costs of regulation. In a 1979 article he said, "It is hard to overestimate the current rapid expansion of government involvement in business in the United States." Yet he seems to have risen to that difficult task, claiming that regulations imposed $100 billion of annual costs on business before the arrival of the Reagan administration. Furthermore, he claimed that four-fifths of federal regulatory budgets were devoted to "the newer areas of social regulation, such as job safety, energy and the environment, and consumer safety and health."[4]

Another economist, William Tabb, examined Weidenbaum's studies and found them to be, in polite terms, shoddy. For example, Weidenbaum counted as "newer areas of social regulation" not only the Food and Drug Administration (created in 1931), but also the Coast Guard, the Customs Service, the Bureau of Alcohol, Tobacco and Firearms, and many other agencies which are neither new nor socially oriented.

Weidenbaum employed a unique "multiplier" method to arrive at his $100 billion figure. He assembled separate estimates of the amounts spent to comply with various agencies' regulations in 1976. The total of these costs was 20 times the budgets of the agencies. So far all later years he simply multiplied the agency budgets by 20 to arrive at the cost of compliance. By including the Coast Guard and the like, he got the agency budget total up to $5 billion by 1979, hence the $100 billion "cost" to business.

Tabb showed that this figure is a wild overstatement. Reorganizing Weidenbaum's data to focus on the 11 social regulatory agencies created since 1960, Tabb found that the costs they imposed on business in 1976 were 6.6 times the agencies' budgets, not 20 times. The 1979 budget total for the 11 agencies was slightly under $1.8 billion, so Weidenbaum's multiplier method implies that the cost to business of the "newer areas of social regulation" was under $12 billion.

Looking at the costs of regulation alone, without considering the benefits—as Weidenbaum and other advocates of deregulation often do—has been compared to "measuring the pain of a hypodermic needle without considering the value of the injected penicillin." Cost-benefit studies, as noted above, have many problems, and tend to ignore the human, nonfinancial benefits of preserving health and safety. Still, for whatever they are worth, there are many studies estimating the economic benefits created by government regulation. A survey of this literature produced a best guess of $21 billion in annual benefits from the Clean Air Act in 1978. A similar figure for water pollution rules was $12 billion, largely reflecting improved recreational use of rivers and lakes. Reductions in deaths due to auto safety standards may be "worth" $6 billion a year, and reduced workplace accidents worth $10 billion. So these four areas alone, which are not the only benefits resulting from the newer regulatory agencies, were estimated to be worth $49 billion a year—more than four times the costs imposed by the whole group of 11 agencies in Tabb's calculation.[5]

The burden of government paperwork has, of course, become legendary among grumbling businessmen. More than a third of Weidenbaum's estimated costs of regulations consist of paperwork done to comply with federal rules. However, the government's 1976 study of paperwork requirements, which Weidenbaum relied on, found that two-thirds of the time spent by all businesses filling out federal forms was due to a single agency, the Federal Communications Commission. The daily logs of programs, operations, and maintenance with the FCC demanded from radio and television stations simply dwarfed the efforts of any other agency.

(Does this sound implausible? It did to me, so I called a radio station manager to check. She confirmed that the FCC did require incredibly detailed daily logs, and was amazed that other industries did not have to keep similar records. Some of the logs, she felt, would be kept by the station for its own records, even without regulations; some were used by the FCC to check on fairness, "equal time" and community service broadcast standards; and some probably fell into the category of silly rules.)

Whether it ever served a useful purpose or not, the huge FCC paperwork load is well on its way into the trashcan of history, as the Reagan administration has moved to deregulate broadcasting. In contrast with the FCC's former appetite for paper, four leading newer agencies (EPA, OSHA, the Consumer Products Safety Commission and the National Highway Traffic Safety Administration) together were responsible for just over one percent of all paperwork required by federal regulators in 1976.[6]

There's no success like failure

Squawking from business and its friends to the contrary, the environmental regulations of the 1970s often led the way to increased profits for the regulated companies. For instance, the ban on fluorocarbon aerosol sprays prompted American Cyanamid's Miss Breck division to develop a new spray can, free of fluorocarbons, that was cheaper than aerosols. Conoco's coal trains used to scatter coal dust over the countryside, losing tons of coal per trainload; pollution controls forced them to stop that loss. Ordered to control air pollution from its factories, General Motors developed new boilers that made the air cleaner and also cut the factories' fuel bills. DuPont used to dump iron chloride wastes into the ocean until the EPA found out about it; now the company reprocesses and sells iron chloride at a profit, just as its competitors had been doing all along.

In at least two cases dire predictions have been made that entire industries would be ruined by regulations—and the industries have gone on to prosper. Polyvinyl chloride (PVC) is one of the most widely used plastics, found in phonograph records, bottles, food wrappings, and hundreds of other common products. It is made from vinyl chloride (VC), a gas which was discovered to be a potent cause of cancer in the early 1970s. OSHA responded by lowering the allowable exposure of workers, formerly 500 parts per million of VC in the air, down to 1 part per million in 1975.

Consulting firms studying the VC standard for OSHA and for the plastics industry predicted that it would cost $90 billion and would lead to the loss of more than two million jobs. Actually, nothing of the sort happened. B.F. Goodrich, a leading producer, developed new production techniques that plugged many leaks and reduced VC waste sharply, for a cost to the company of only $34 million. Moreover, Goodrich found that the new techniques cut labor costs, and could be leased to other companies. From 1975 to 1978, the VC/PVC industry grew more than twice as fast as U.S. manufacturing in general, and four major new producers entered the market.

Similarly, the EPA feared that its tough standards limiting the dumping of toxic wastes into municipal waterworks could put as many as 20% of all electroplating firms out of business. But again, the regulation forced the development of new methods of recycling wastes. One Milwaukee electroplating company found that the equipment needed to comply with the toxic waste standard would pay for itself in recycled water and chemicals within 2½ years.[7]

Environmental regulations, of course, are not just good for particular businesses. They are also responsible for noticeable reduction in some (not all) forms of air and water pollution. During the 1970s particulate emissions (soot, dust, etc.) in the air fell by one-half, and sulfur dioxide by one-sixth. The newest cars were much cleaner than their predecessors; even the average pollution per mile, for all old and new cars on the road, dropped by one-third to one-half over the decade.

Bodies of water such as Lake Erie, the Willamette River in Oregon, the Detroit River, the Connecticut River and many others, saw increasing signs of life, reversing the trend of earlier years. The Cuyahoga River in Cleveland was no longer capable of catching fire, as it once did. While pollution was by no means defeated in the 1970s, it was definitely pushed back—by some of the regulations that are now under the sharpest attack.

In short, the newer areas of regulation are producing monetary benefits worth many times their cost, imposing no significant paperwork burden on business, stimulating profitable new innovations, and achieving measurable success in reducing pollution. Why, then, are so many people saying such terrible things about these rules?

The question can be answered on several levels. Most immediately, many regulations do not lead the affected companies into more profitable methods of production. A corporation forced to control air pollution from its factories will gain little comfort from the knowledge that the health benefits to society outweigh the costs of anti-pollution devices. The costs show up on the company's balance sheet; the benefits do not. What is true for society as a whole, therefore—that the benefits are greater than the cost of controls—is not true for the corporations that must install the controls. Yet, in a private enterprise system, society can only achieve these benefits by forcing business to invest in health and safety.

Beyond the immediate threat of any particular regulation, there is the general problem for business that if regulations are accepted as legitimate and useful, they will continue to spread. New standards for pollution control, for product safety, for occupational health, will keep on cropping up. Even if your company has not yet been harmed by such rules, you may want to join the crusade against regulation as a form of insurance policy for the future.

Going still further in this direction, rhetoric about the failure of regulation sometimes conceals a deep-seated fear of the very fact of regulatory success. The belief that all social problems are solved best by the market, that businesses must be left free to do as they choose, is an article of faith for the right wing. What greater heresy could be imagined than the idea that corporations create problems and the federal government is reasonably effective in solving them? If this notion catches on, it may not stop with things like pollution: voters may demand controls on prices, standards for socially useful investments, workplace democracy... clearly, a dangerous line of thought. Better to head it off before it starts, by claiming that even the controls on pollution were unsuccessful and ill-advised. Thus there is widespread support in the business world for the general goal of deregulation, if not for the specific doctrines of supply-side theory. There is much less support, however, among the voters.

Add five jiggers and stir

> Look what happened to Germany in the 1930s. The dignity of man was subordinated to the powers of Nazism. The dignity of man was subordinated in Russia... Those are the forces that this thing [environmentalism] can evolve into.
>
> —Former Interior Secretary James Watt[8]

James Watt had an inspired style of public relations, which led to his amazing fall from grace in 1983. Who else could have displayed such a flair for insulting blacks, women, Jews, cripples and Beach Boys fans? But as Interior Secretary, his deepest and wildest hosility was directed at the environmental movement— and at the environment.

Watt had good reason to sound a bit hysterical about environmentalism. By an impressively wide margin, the public did not share his enthusiasm for unleashing corporate polluters.

A 1983 public opinion poll done for *Business Week* (and reported by the magazine in a slightly anxious tone) found 86% or more opposed to any relaxation in clean air, water, or hazardous waste disposal standards. Several stereotypes were punctured by the poll: union members, like the rest of the public, believed strongly in enforcing air pollution laws. even if factories were forced to shut down as a result; Western states, sometimes thought to be a stronghold of Reaganism, were more adamant than the rest of the country in supporting clean air and water.[9]

While a majority of those polled approved of the work of environmental organizations, only 25% felt that the Reagan administration or U.S. industry were doing a good job in combatting pollution. This skepticism about government and industry is well-founded, as the 1983 dioxin scandals demonstrated.

Dioxin is one of the most deadly substances ever created. One-millionth of an ounce is enough to kill a chicken. Significant increases in cancer show up when rats are fed doses as low as five parts per *trillion*. This is an almost incomprehensibly low level; martini drinkers may be interested to know that it is equivalent to five jiggers of vermouth in one million railroad tank cars of gin.

Dioxin is an unavoidable byproduct in the manufacture of hexachlorophene, a once-popular antiseptic, and of 2,4,5-T (Agent Orange), a chemical used extensively as a weedkiller in this country and as a weapon to defoliate the countryside in Vietnam. The minute traces of dioxin found in Agent Orange are widely believed to be the cause of the high rates of birth defects, cancer and other diseases among Vietnam veterans (and among the people of Vietnam) who were in the defoliated areas. And chemical industry wastes containing dioxin, one of the worst pollutants at Love Canal in New York, were also the cause of the evacuation of several Missouri towns in 1983.

The dangers of dioxin are no recent discovery, at least not to everyone involved. Back in 1965 Dow Chemical, the leading manufacturer of 2,4,5-T, invited researchers from other companies to an unusual secret meeting about dioxin. According to participants in the meeting, Dow presented its findings of serious liver damage and other problems caused by dioxin, and stressed that it did not want the information made public because the situation might "explode" and lead to new government regulations.[10]

New regulations did eventually appear, but at somewhat less than explosive speed. In 1972 the use of hexachlorophene was restricted, but not entirely banned; the last plant making the chemical was not closed until 1983 (and then by New Jersey officials, not by federal regulators).[11]

Meanwhile, the Missouri dioxin crisis, in which it appears that dozens of towns or neighborhoods may be unsafe to live in, can be traced back to another plant which once made hexachlorophene. It sold its wastes, including a sludge containing dioxin, to a salvage oil dealer. The oil dealer mixed the sludge with waste oil and sprayed it on dirt roads and fields for dust control. The owner of a horse ranch whose grounds had been sprayed noticed in 1971 that something was killing her horses in alarming numbers. By 1974 dioxin had been identified as the culprit. After that it took the ranch owner only eight more years to get the EPA and the Missouri Division of Health interested in the case.[12]

The same breathtaking pace was applied to regulation of 2,4,5-T, once widely used as a weedkiller. Due to the growing awareness of the dioxin in 2,4,5-T, the EPA banned most but not all uses of the chemical in 1979. Extensive use was still allowed on rice fields and cattle grazing lands. The EPA also began administrative hearings to determine whether the ban should be extended or scaled back. Those hearings were still going on when Ronald Reagan was inaugurated in January 1981.

The deregulators of the 1980s moved faster than the regulators of the 1970s. In February 1981, after only one month in office, representatives of Reagan's EPA asked for a recess in the hearings on 2,4,5-T to allow negotiations with Dow Chemical. An EPA staff report stressing the dangers of dioxin was suppressed in July 1981. By early 1983, the EPA and Dow were said to be close to an agreement that would have weakened the 1979 ban and allowed increased use of 2,4,5-T.[13]

This style of deregulation, fortunately, does not fool all of the people all of the time. Word of corruption at the EPA began to leak out in 1983, and the issues in the "Sewergate" controversy included the EPA's excessive coziness with Dow Chemical and corresponding disinterest in dioxin. Rita Lavelle, formerly in charge of the government's effort to clean up toxic waste dumps, met with Dow executives more than once a month during her tenure in office. Lower-level EPA staffers complained that top agency officials (presumably Lavelle and/or Anne Gorsuch Burford, former head of the EPA) ordered changes in a report on dioxin to make Dow happier. The key change was the deletion of the conclusion about wastes from Dow's Midland, Michigan plant: "Dow's discharge represented the major source, if not the only source, of TCDD [dioxin] contamination" found in nearby bodies of water, according to the uncensored version.[14] Lavelle and Burford were forced out of the EPA by the public scandal; some months later Dow announced that it had grown tired of the controversy and was quitting production of 2,4,5-T. The lengthy regulatory delays had, however, given Dow time to sell off its large inventory of the chemical, and to shut down production on a schedule of its own choosing.[15]

The good, the bad and the oily

Even bigger battles over deregulation are underway elsewhere. The heaviest impact of environmental regulation falls on the energy industry. While investments required for pollution control amounted to $7 billion for business as a whole in 1979, $4 billion of that total was spent by public utilities and the petroleum industry. Pollution control spending was over 8% of new investment in the energy industry, twice the level for industry as a whole.[16]

For the energy industry, the stakes are far higher than a mere $4 billion a year. They are seeking the "freedom," formerly denied to them, to drill oil and gas, strip-mine coal, and build pipelines, power plants and refineries wherever they want, whatever the environmental impact—a freedom which means many billions for them, and disaster for the air-breathing, water-drinking public.

Long accustomed to advance planning, the oil industry got its regulatory wish list for the Reagan years written up ahead of time. Back in August 1980, the American Petroleum Institute— Big Oil's lobbying and public relations outfit—published *Two Energy Futures*, their plan for the 1980s.[17] While no direct pipeline from the oilmen to the Reagan adminstration has yet been uncovered, the API's plan bore an uncanny resemblance to the policies of the Interior Department under James Watt.

The API's "two energy futures" are the bad one, in which the country continues to import more and more OPEC oil, and the good one, in which the energy industry is given free rein to produce more oil, gas and coal in the U.S. Two major recommendations are offered about how to achieve the good future instead of the bad one. First, open up federal lands and the federally controlled Outer Continental Shelf for more oil and gas drilling and coal mining. Second, make environmental regulations more flexible; the Clean Air Act, in particular, is targetted for intensive flexing.

The API sees the problem in supply-side terms: how can we boost the domestic supply of energy? Although U.S. oil and gas output declined throughout the 1970s, the API believes that more rapid exploration would at least maintain 1980 production levels. And the oilmen, who own many of the largest coal companies, are especially bullish on coal ouput. They hope to double 1980 levels by 1990. Put this together with modest contributions from nuclear power, synthetic fuels, renewable energy sources and conservation, and sure enough, only about half the 1980 level of oil imports would be needed by 1990.

In the search for oil and gas, much of the U.S. has been exhaustively explored. One-fifth of the country's total land area is either producing oil and gas or under lease for exploration. At least 2,500,000 wells have been drilled, with an average of 2.5 wells per square mile in Texas and 4.5 in Oklahoma.

One big, relatively underexplored area is the land belonging to the federal government. It amounts to one-third of the land area of the U.S., mostly in western states and Alaska. In addition, federally controlled offshore (continental shelf) areas are almost as large as the onshore holdings. As of 1980 the U.S. Geological Survey guessed that federally controlled areas contained 37% of the country's undiscovered oil, almost all offshore, and 43% of the undiscovered natural gas, half of it offshore.

The federal share of coal reserves is similar: about 40% lie on public lands. Most eastern coal is privately owned, but in the West, the API claims the federal government owns 60% of the coal and controls access to another 20% due to the checkerboard pattern of land ownership. Industry hopes for expansion center on western coal because more of it can be strip-mined—a faster, cheaper method than underground mining—and because the United Mine Workers are weaker in the West.

So in oil, gas and coal the federal government controls a lot of what's left in the ground. In order to free you from oil imports, the energy companies plan to free you from a lot of those federal lands.

Despite the reluctance taxpayers may feel about turning national parks, prairies, forests and coastal waters over to Exxon and friends, the API assures us that strip-mining is often good for the countryside: "In many instances, reclamation has improved the quality of the land after it has been surface-mined." In reality, the reforms of the 1970s had barely begun to control the devastation caused by strip-mining, only to be abruptly reversed in 1981. Under Reagan, the Office of Surface Mining, according to one of its officials, became "totally a captive of the mining interests. There are no inspectors out in the field now; they only inspect in response to citizen complaints... I have seen moonscapes on mine sites."[18]

In the arid plains where Western coal is found, quick or careless strip-mining can cause irreversible destruction of topsoil or pollution of the underground water table, ruining the land for agriculture. Scarce water supplies are already the focus of intense political conflict in the region; one study found that in many Western coal deposits, there is no known way to protect the water table during stripping, and therefore "surface mining will inevitably endanger the long-term productivity of an area for a cash crop of coal that can be harvested only once."[19]

One might expect that such problems, combined with the energy glut and recession of the early 1980s, would slow down the leasing of federal coal. But James Watt was a man in a hurry. As well as stepping up the rate of offshore oil leasing, Watt boasted that he leased 800% more coal in 1981 and 1982 than the Carter administration did in the preceding two years. In the Powder River Basin in Wyoming, where huge amounts of coal were leased in April 1982, the Interior Department received $100 million less than fair market value, according to the federal General Accounting Office. The depressed revenue was due not only to low coal prices during the energy glut, but also to Watt's novel practice of telling coal companies the lowest price the government would accept in advance of the bidding. Moreover, 8 of the 11 tracts received only one bid, adding to the sense that something other than competitive market forces was at work.[20]

With all deliberate delay

While one could dwell further on the problems of energy production on federal lands—offshore drilling accidents, for instance, could wipe out fishing, tourism and recreation in coastal areas—there is another side to the push for deregulation. Not only the extraction of oil, gas and coal, but also the use of these fuels is hemmed in by government restrictions. The plans of the energy industry for burning fossil fuels run smack into the Clean Air Act and other limits on pollution.

Some corporate spokesmen rant and rave about pollution controls. An official of the National Association of Manufacturers fumes that clean air standards seem designed "for the 90 year old jogger with tuberculosis."[21] But the well-oiled publicity apparatus of the petroleum industry avoids such crudeness. It's just wonderful that we've come so far in cleaning up the environment, gushes the API; in fact, we're doing so well that surely we can afford to be reasonable, to compromise, to balance the goal of further environmental progress against the need for energy development...

For the top target of all this reasonableness, the Clean Air Act, the oilmen support any of a number of intricate amendments—the effect of which would be to allow more air pollution in many areas. Also in need of creative reinterpretation are the Safe Drinking Water Act, the Endangered Species Act, and many more. According to the API, environmental laws have caused lengthy delays or cancellations of power plants, pipelines, oil terminals, refineries and other energy projects.

Not all compromises are reasonable, however; not all cancellations and delays are regrettable. The environmental movement has thus far blocked attempts at weakening the Clean Air Act, without causing any visible energy crisis. In fact, there are three major reasons why the controls on air pollution should be made stronger, despite the limits those controls impose on energy development.

First and most important, crud in the air makes people sick. Many air pollutants increase the rate of emphysema, bronchitis and other lung diseases. Cancers of the lung and throat are more common in urban, industrial communities than in rural ones; a number of cancers are particularly frequent in areas near petroleum refineries and petrochemical plants.[22] The progress in pollution control during the 1970s only began to alleviate these problems—but the energy industry would have us believe that we have come so far that we can now afford some backsliding.

Second, fossil fuel burning causes acid rain. Coal is the worst offender, per unit of energy. Sulfur dioxide and nitrogen oxides, released out of the smokestack when coal is burned, form sulfuric and nitric acids on contact with the moisture in the atmosphere.

The result is that highly acidic rain falls on regions downwind from coal-burning areas. Acid rain not only kills fish and plant life; since it falls into metropolitan reservoirs, it corrodes urban water pipes and can cause health problems as well. Acid rain has already reached serious levels in the eastern United States and Canada.[23]

Finally, increases in carbon dioxide in the atmosphere contribute to the "greenhouse effect." Again, any fossil fuel is part of the problem, but coal is the worst. The greenhouse effect is the reason your car heats up if you leave it in the sun with the windows rolled up. Light passes easily through the glass; on striking something inside, like car seats, most of the light is converted into heat, which can't escape through the glass nearly as fast as light comes in. (That's why greenhouses are warmer than the outside air, too.) Carbon dioxide in the atmosphere acts like window glass, letting in light but holding onto heat. Thus too much fossil fuel burning could heat up the atmosphere and cause massive shifts in climate, perhaps melting the polar ice caps and flooding coastal regions. It is still uncertain how fast this will happen, but it is clear that the level of carbon dioxide in the air is going up.[24]

Refineries and power plants are cheaper to build without pollution controls. But the eventual costs to the public are much greater than the costs of doing it right in the first place. Also, to cite a favorite industry complaint, there is no evidence that pollution controls have made coal-fired power plants uncompetitive. Throughout the 1970s, as tough controls were implemented, the cost of coal-burning plants did, of course, rise. But the cost of the major commercial alternative, nuclear power, rose much faster—even before Three Mile Island.[25] In other words, clean uses of coal, though expensive, are cheaper than the ever-more-costly quest for safe uses of uranium.

Much as the utilities have belly-ached about it, some of the construction delays caused by government regulation have, in retrospect, been good for corporate finances. When prices of all forms of energy began to shoot up after the oil crisis of 1973-74, businesses and households moved rapidly and apparently permanently toward energy conservation. On average, the U.S. now uses 18% less energy per dollar of GNP (corrected for inflation) than it did in 1973, and there is plenty of room for even more conservation.[26] This has meant little or no need for new capacity to generate electricity.

Yet for years after the first oil crisis, utilities insisted on ignoring the shift toward conservation, overestimating the demand for electricity, and consequently trying to build unecessary, expensive plants. A little more obstructionist regulation could have saved some companies even more, as the unhappy owners of various partially-completed nuclear power plants could tell you.

In the Northwest, the Washington Public Power Supply System (WPPSS), now commonly known as "whoops," started to build five nuclear power plants in the 1970s, and borrowed more than $8 billion on the bond market to pay for them. But collapsing demand for electricity led to the cancellation of two partially built plants in 1982, and indefinite postponement of two of the remaining three. In effect WPPSS had spent billions digging now-worthless holes in the ground. And the repayment of the bonds which had financed this upscale ditch-digging would have imposed intolerably high rates on WPPSS customers. In 1983 WPPSS set a record for the largest default in the history of the municipal bond market.[27]

A defender of the industry might object that the demand for electricity collapsed, WPPSS went broke, and conservation became an attractive alternative, in large part because government regulation drove up the price of energy. But if truly clean, safe energy production is more expensive than conservation, then it is reasonable, from the point of view of society as a whole, to conserve. Unregulated energy production might look cheaper still, but only because of the failure to count the hidden costs of more destruction of public lands, more disease, more devastation of the air and water.

Take a good look . . .

The dioxin scandals and the battles over energy industry pollution are only two examples, though two of the most important, of the corporate stake in Reagan's push for deregulation. The supply-side rationale, even if no longer widely believed, helped advance key items on the business agenda. The deregulatory campaign has extended from the vast issues raised by the oil industry to the specific contents of the smallest consumer products—or, one might say, from the slime to the ridiculous.

Finally, therefore, consider the common chicken. Have you ever wondered what the label "USDA inspected and passed" on a supermarket chicken package really means? You would probably guess that someone from the Department of Agriculture has looked at that chicken. And, in a certain sense, you would be right.

Actually, chickens move by a federal inspector on a conveyor belt, or "disassembly line." The inspector looks at both sides of a chicken with the aid of mirrors, and then tells a packinghouse worker where to trim away any unacceptable meat. It is not an unreasonable-sounding procedure—depending on the speed of the line. In the good old days, a decade or so ago, chickens were allowed to move by the inspectors at a rate of 45 birds per minute. The inspector thus had a full 1 1/3 seconds to devote to each chicken. During the Carter administration, the permissible line speed was raised to 70 per minute, or more than one every second.

At such speeds, inspectors often cannot help falling into a drowsy state of "line-hypnosis" in which, to quote an Illinois poultry inspector, "Birds affected with cancerous tissue...are being missed and not condemned as required by regulation." But, not to be outdone by the wimps of the Carter era, Reagan's deregulators proposed to rev up the line to 105 birds per minute, almost two every second.[28] As the chickens fly by the inspectors at near-highway speeds, the resulting quality of inspection is unfortunately easy to imagine.

Next time you buy a chicken, take a close look at it. There's a good chance that no one else has.

chapter 5

the
economics
of
the
apocalypse

*...the second half of the Administration's program to
revitalize America.*
—Defense Secretary Caspar Weinberger

*...nothing less than a conscious commitment to beat
our plowshares into swords.*
—Congressman Ronald Dellums

Ronald Dellums and Caspar Weinberger are both right. The
Reagan administration is beating our plowshares into swords,
shifting public funds from peaceful to warlike purposes as fast as
Congress will allow. And the administration is also relying on
military spending to help revitalize the economy. Neither of the
other two major strands of Reaganomics can do the job: supply-
side theory had barely accomplished its mission of slashing taxes
and regulations before it flamed out in a blaze of Laffer Curves
and arithmetic mistakes; monetarism, committed to some less
spectacular mistakes of its own (about which more in the next
chapter), offers nothing but years of high unemployment as the
cure for inflation. Alone among Reagan's policies, the boost in
the Pentagon budget directly creates jobs and stimulates production. Regrettably, it might also incinerate the human race.

One of the lessons of the Great Depression of the 1930s was that private business on its own does not reliably provide anything close to full employment. The British economist John Maynard Keynes became famous for proposing deficit spending as a solution to massive unemployment, and for developing an economic theory which explained why it worked. Less well known is Keynes' grudging awareness of the way in which his ideas would be carried out.

> It is, it seems, politically impossible for a capitalistic democracy to organize expenditure on the scale necessary to make the grand experiment which would prove my case—except in war conditions.[1]

Events proved Keynes' cynicism partially correct. The official unemployment rate remained above 14% throughout the 1930s; it was World War II, not the New Deal or the impact of Keynesian ideas, which ended the depression. After the war, military spending stayed high (a brief interlude in the late 1940s aside), under the successive impact of the Korean War, the Cold War, and the fighting in Indochina. Keynesian policy has always been, to a signficant extent, "military Keynesianism." Under Ronald Reagan, it has become much more so.

As noted in Chapter 1, other areas of government grew more rapidly than the Pentagon during the 1960s and 1970s. By the late 1970s the military absorbed "only" about one-fourth of federal spending. Still, the Pentagon was the nation's largest employment agency, with 3% of the labor force on its payroll—2% in uniform, 1% in civilian jobs at the Defense Department. In addition, military purchases of goods and services from private contractors accounted for about another 3% of GNP.[2] So the military and its suppliers employed something like 6% of us, even before the Reagan buildup.

Viewed as insurance against depressions, the role of the military is even larger. In a situation like the 1930s, a program that provided direct employment for 6% of the labor force would cause a surge in consumer spending. Formerly unemployed people, receiving paychecks from the Pentagon or from Lockheed, would go out and spend more money. Industries making consumer goods would then hire more workers, who in turn would spend more money, and so on. Ultimately, direct employment for

6% of the labor force would create indirect employment for roughly another 6%. So if the alternative was sinking into depression, the military budget of the late 1970s was responsible, directly and indirectly, for about 12% of all employment.

(Notice that this figure is crucially dependent on what the alternative was. If the alternative was a program providing full employment in nonmilitary activities, then the Pentagon was simply taking 6% of the labor force away from peaceful pursuits, not increasing total employment at all.)

Critics have often argued that military spending provides fewer jobs and less technological progress than other programs would. For instance, one study found that transferring 30% of the Pentagon budget to education, health, welfare and environmental programs would increase both output and employment by 2%. Seymour Melman and others have suggested that the concentration of the nation's research and development effort on weapons industries is responsible for the lack of productivity growth in civilian manufacturing over the last decade.[3] As far as most of us are concerned, such statements are certainly true. It is easy to imagine programs that could produce more jobs and technological progress for the same amount of money. Equally important, these alternatives would pose less of a threat to human life.

But from the point of view of business, military spending is more attractive then most other government programs. Some government activities would compete with private industry; more mass transit or public housing would not help the auto or private housing industries. And too much social welfare spending, of course, weakens the "work incentives" so popular with employers.

The Pentagon does none of this, but instead creates new industries, such as aerospace, and profitable sidelines for many other manufacturers. As Chrysler sank ever deeper into the red in the late 1970s, its most reliable source of profits was the division that produced the M-1 tank. (By 1982, however, Chrysler had to sell its tank division in the quest for cash to cover its auto losses.)

In terms of technological progress, other programs might theoretically do even better than military spending. But it should be remembered that the Pentagon was largely responsible for the birth of the semiconductor and computer industries in the 1950s, and even today continues to spur further advances in these fast-moving fields. From the largest supercomputers to the next generation of microprocessor chips, the winds of war are propelling everyone's favorite high-technology industry.[4]

Military production is also quite profitable. Solid figures are hard to find, but it appears reasonable to guess that military contracts accounted for 8% or more of total corporate profits, even in the late 1970s.[5] For the leading defense contractors, of course, Pentagon-sponsored profits were much more important. It is not surprising that these firms have joined with the top brass of the Armed Forces to form a powerful, successful lobby for the continuation and expansion of their favorite weapons systems.

The military is not the only program to offer many of these advantages to businessmen. Shooting expensive rockets into outer space meets most of the same criteria quite nicely, even guaranteeing profits to some of the same corporations, and has indeed been tried at times. No way has been found, however, to attach the same moral urgency to improvements in our knowledge of astronomy as to safeguards against the Red Menace. Thus space exploration, a much smaller program to begin with, has won only modest budget increases under Reagan. The only NASA program that enjoys Pentagon-style affluence is the space shuttle, prized for its ability to launch military satellites.

Whether the Reaganauts realize it or not (some do and some don't), the moral imperative they attach to military spending is essential to their economic program. It allows them to prattle on about the virtues of reducing the role of government without having to carry it out across the board. Theory to the contrary, boosts in one major area of public spending remain legitimate, almost sacred, in their eyes.

The very size of the military budgets projected for the next few years indicates that top White House advisors never took Reagan's rhetoric seriously. If supply-side theory had worked, if the tax cut and deregulation had sent production soaring, then military and civilian industry would have ended up competing for limited supplies of investment funds and productive facilities. The rosiest official forecasts of recovery have thus predicted that some civilian investments will have to be postponed or cancelled in the mid-1980s to accomodate the military boom.[6]

More realistically, as supply-side theory has sputtered out, military Keynesianism has been needed to keep the economy moving. Like the Great Depression of the 1930s, the near-great slump of the early 1980s may be ended in large part by preparations for war. In this scenario, unlike the more glowing predictions, an internal logic can be found in Reaganomics. Perhaps the Pentagon budget was designed as a safety net to catch falling economic advisors.

The balance of terror

Military Keynesianism would be a bizarre and wasteful, but otherwise harmless economic strategy—if we could be promised that the weapons involved would never be used. No such promise, though, has been offered. Indeed, the rapid expansion of the Pentagon budget is typically justified on military rather than economic grounds.

Above all, our growing military establishment is said to be protecting us from the Soviet Threat. As in the 1950s and early 1960s, many Americans have been convinced that our country is in danger—in which case, expensive as it may be, the military buildup would seem to have a powerful rationale. Discussion of the Pentagon budget must therefore focus on questions of security. Do we need to spend $245 billion in 1984 and $323 billion in 1986, as the Reagan administration proposes, to keep us safe in today's world? Do we need our present level of armaments and more to defend ourselves from the Russians?

The most basic military reality is the nuclear balance of terror. Either the U.S. or the U.S.S.R. is capable of bombing the other side back into the Stone Age, as a U.S. general once advocated during the Vietnam war. We are, in fact, in the lead in this particular race: depending on whose estimates you believe, we have 9,000 to 10,000 strategic nuclear weapons ("strategic" means long-range ones capable of hitting the opposing super-power), and our NATO allies have another 1,000, against the Soviet Union's 7,000 to 8,000. But both sides have more than enough.

In the past, military planners assumed that the very balance of terror would provide a grim assurance of peace. The doctrine known as "mutual assured destruction" (MAD) said that since both sides know they would be destroyed by a major war, neither side will start one. Then, barring a computer malfunction or the ascent to power of a madman on one side or the other (events which unfortunately are all too possible), we are more or less safe.

More recently, the advocates of a new U.S. buildup in nuclear weaponry have claimed that MAD is no longer valid.

Soviet military power was said to be advancing so rapidly that a "window of vulnerability" would soon open—a period of a few years in the late 1980s when the Soviet Union would be able to launch a crippling "first strike," taking us by surprise and destroying so many of our weapons that we would be unable to counterattack. New U.S. weapons, particularly the MX, were needed to strengthen our defenses and close the window of vulnerability.

The window of vulnerability appeared to be official U.S. military doctrine from the beginning of the Reagan administration, right up to April 11, 1983. That was the date on which the final report was issued by the President's commission to find a home for the MX. The commission had been appointed to repair a major defect in the window of vulnerability theory: the MX had to be kept somewhere secure enough to withstand a Soviet first strike and threaten to counterattack; otherwise the MX, like all our other missiles, could be wiped out by the sneaky commies.

After four months of failing to find a sufficiently secure site, the commission gave up and in effect said, what the hell, put them in the same old missile silos we've already been using; the Russians could never really knock out everything we've got at once.[7] It was the same old MAD tune that previous administrations had been singing for years. Ronald Reagan accepted the commission's report in its entirety, thus quietly slamming shut the window of vulnerability. Only the justification for the MX was gone, however; the missile itself lived on, as did other proposed advances in nuclear hardware.

However flimsy its basis in reality, the supposed threat of a Soviet first strike was used by the Reagan administration to justify a chilling change in U.S. military posture. Top officials no longer seem to think that U.S. use of nuclear weapons is quite as unthinkable as it used to be. Vice President George Bush has asserted that a "limited nuclear war" is winnable. Former Secretary of State Alexander Haig claimed that there were worse things than nuclear war, and managed to terrify millions of people on both sides of the Atlantic by casually mentioning the possibility of exploding a nuclear "warning shot" over Europe if conventional war breaks out.

In fact, it may not be the Soviet Union which is close to achieving a first strike capability. Wiping out the other country's entire arsenal before it can be used is a more technologically sophisticated task than simply causing unacceptable levels of mass murder. The MAD strategy could employ big, dirty missiles with relatively sloppy guidance systems, of the sort which both the U.S. and the U.S.S.R. have in abundance: no great accuracy is required to ruin a metropolitan area with a hydrogen bomb.

But a first strike would require pinpoint accuracy to blow up hardened missile silos, and a means of locating and destroying missile-launching submarines at sea. And in such high-technology forms of destruction the U.S. is far ahead—as argued in *First Strike!*, by Robert Aldridge, a former design engineer for the Polaris and Trident missile systems.[8] By the late 1980s, missiles such as the MX and the Trident II, guided by powerful on-board computer circuits and radio signals from navigational satellites, will be able to land quite precisely on Soviet missile silos and destroy them. (This new generation of U.S. missiles will have warheads with comparatively low explosive yields. But smaller warheads will be more than made up for by greater accuracy in guidance systems—a fact overlooked in simple comparisons of U.S. vs. Soviet megatonnage.) Likewise, a network of U.S. satellite-, ship- and land-based weapons systems, coupled to some of the world's largest supercomputers, may soon be able to scan the oceans, locate the entire Soviet submarine fleet, and sink it. The Soviet Union might eventually catch up, but at present it lags far behind in these computerized styles of war. The window of vulnerability in the late 1980s is not opening on us.

The threat of a first strike by either side upsets the balance of terror on which MAD precariously rested. The weaker side, fearing destruction of its arsenal, must "use it or lose it" in a crisis. Paradoxically, our possession of a first strike capability could goad the U.S.S.R. into striking first.

With such uplifting thoughts in the air, government officials have begun to address the problems of postwar life. T.K. Jones, deputy undersecretary of defense for strategic and nuclear forces, believes it would take only two to four years for the United States to fully recover from an all-out nuclear attack. The Federal Emergency Management Agency, which is in charge of civil defense, cheerfully claims, "Even under the worst circumstances imaginable there would be no danger of a repetition of the bubonic plague that devastated Europe in the mid-14th century." The agency recommends that you build a "pre-planned snack bar shelter" in your basement, which can double as an entertainment center before and, conceivably, after the attack.

Planning for America after the apocalypse has reached impressive levels of detail. The Postal Service has prepared Emergency Change of Address Cards (Form 809) for use following a nuclear attack. The Treasury Department warns banks to expect the bond market to be temporarily depressed. The IRS will forgive all back taxes, since its computerized records will presumably be destroyed. One weak spot is the Public Health Service, which apparently has not updated its plan for "sanitary aspects of disposal of the dead" since 1956. (The 1956 plan recommended digging large ditches.) Through it all, civil defense director William Chipman offers his confidence that the survivors "would in all probability rise to the occasion and restore some kind of a country that would fairly be called the post-attack United States...As I say, ants will eventually build another anthill."[9]

Ants, however, are distinctly more likely to survive than human beings, as insects have proved able to withstand doses of radioactivity that are lethal to mammals. In short, it appears that a war that could end human life on earth is becoming a live option for Ronald Reagan's Pentagon planners. At this point there is no longer any meaning to winning or losing on the battlefield; the only victory we can survive is success in nuclear disarmament.

The CIA's Soviet budgets

The U.S. is sometimes said to be dangerously behind in conventional, non-nuclear forces—a claim which rests on a variety of misunderstandings. The Soviet armed forces do have many more active duty personnel, but large numbers are occupied with jobs done by civilians in the U.S., with internal security or with defending the border with China. The U.S. has felt no comparable need to put hundreds of thousands of soldiers along the Canadian or Mexican border. As a result, the two superpowers have approximately equal numbers of troops available for the titanic Central European battle which looms so large in the minds of our military planners. In addition, our European allies have much larger armies than theirs do. Total NATO troops available for war in Europe well outnumber their Warsaw Pact counterparts.[10]

The Soviet lead in conventional military hardware also looks much less ominous on close inspection. They have a larger number of ships, but we have a greater tonnage of ships and more naval firepower. Moreover, our naval forces were growing faster, even before the Reagan buildup: a Library of Congress study found that the U.S. and its allies built 200 warships in the 1970s, versus only 109 built by the Warsaw Pact.[11]

Likewise, they have more tanks, but recent Middle East wars have shown tanks to be increasingly vulnerable to "smart" (computer-guided) weapons, an area in which we are years ahead. Planes and anti-aircraft defense, too, can be knocked out with smart weapons, as demonstrated in Israel's 1982 invasion of Lebanon: Israeli armed forces equipped with the latest U.S. electronic gadgetry absolutely crushed the Syrians, who were using the latest Soviet gear. Even the Soviet Union's 1983 shooting of a South Korean passenger airliner, while morally outrageous, was not particularly a sign of strength. Western military analysts were amazed at how clumsy and slow-moving Soviet air defenses turned out to be, even around a top-secret missile test site.[12]

All in all, the Soviet military apparatus is capable of defending its own borders, or invading a small country like Afghanistan (though unable to pacify it). There is no evidence that it threatens the United States or Western Europe.

Much has been made of the supposed increases in Soviet military spending in recent years. Ronald Reagan never tires of claiming that the U.S.S.R. outspent us by hundreds of billions of dollars in the 1970s. The CIA, the agency in charge of making up these numbers, has produced estimates as high as $420 billion for the military spending gap from 1971 through 1980. However, such numbers are figments of the CIA's statistical imagination.

There are some genuine problems in comparing Soviet and U.S. budgets. Merely converting rubles to dollars at the current exchange rate may be misleading because the patterns of prices are so different. For example, comparisons of consumer incomes are hard to interpret because Soviet cars and other consumer goods are very expensive by U.S. standards, while medical care is free and housing and mass transit are very cheap. Similar problems hamper the comparison of military budgets.

Faced with this statistical difficulty, the CIA arbitrarily employs a method which is sure to exaggerate Soviet spending. The CIA catalogues all the equipment and labor used by the Soviet military, and then calculates what it would cost to buy the same things in the U.S. Soviet tanks are assumed to cost whatever the Pentagon is paying for tanks; Soviet draftees are assumed to be receiving U.S. volunteer army pay rates; and so on. The use of U.S. pay rates, in particular, swells the supposed Soviet budget, since their military apparatus is more labor-intensive, and their soldiers' wages far lower than ours.

Yet another problem with the CIA calculation is that, even on its own terms, it only works as long as you forget about Europe. Again, our Western European allies have much larger military budgets than the Soviet Union's Eastern European ones. Even using the CIA method of calculation, U.S. pay rates and all, total NATO military spending for the 1970s was $300 billion greater than the Warsaw Pact total.[13]

The best-made planes...

In short, a good Soviet threat is hard to find. Yet anti-Soviet rhetoric has justified the colossal, and now rapidly growing, expense of our military establishment, the unparalleled repository of the waste which Ronald Reagan promised to eliminate from federal government. Some of it would be amusing, if it wasn't our money; the Navy buys shipboard tape recorders which cost 47 times as much as equivalent civilian models.[14]

Or there is the Army's latest armored personnel carrier, once scheduled to be delivered by 1965. Fifteen years and many expensive modifications later, a prototype of the allegedly amphibious Infantry Fighting Vehicle (IFV) was unveiled. The Wall Street Journal described the scene:

> In the summer of 1980, the cavalry proudly rolled out its version of the IFV for testing in front of Maj. Gen. Louis Wagner, other dignitaries and a local television crew at Fort Knox. It drove into the Ohio River and promptly sank. Something was wrong with a latch related to a rubberized nylon collar that should allow the vehicle to float.
>
> The embarrassment was nothing compared to the uproar the following December when it was reported that the total cost of the IFV program had risen from $7.4 billion to more than $13 billion in one year.[15]

Now renamed the Bradley Fighting Vehicle, it finally rolled into active duty in 1983. Congressional critics were rude enough to point out that it still did not always float.

To see money being wasted in truly grand style, however, you have to look at bigger weapons programs—like Air Force fighter planes. "Tactical Air" squadrons, those planes not intended for nuclear assault on the Soviet Union, were one of the military growth areas of the late 1970s, in some years swallowing as much as a quarter of the entire Pentagon budget. That money was spent on the latest, most complex and most expensive planes, like the F-15, at $40 million each—planes whose great cost is due to exotic capabilities which almost certainly will never be used.

One of the quickest ways to make a plane expensive is to demand that it go faster. A plane designed to fly above twice the speed of sound (Mach 2) cannot be made out of anything as common as aluminum. Materials such as titanium, stainless steel and beryllium, none of them cheap, are required for the airframe. The engines also must be bigger and more complex, and must be made of more costly materials.

But, as one of the most important Pentagon leaks of recent years revealed, in actual wars pilots do not fly at these speeds. In the Vietnam war, U.S. pilots flew more than 100,000 flights in planes capable of exceeding Mach 2. Only one instance of a few seconds above Mach 1.6 was ever recorded. Only a total of a few minutes of flight time even reached Mach 1.4. Moreover, supersonic flight burns fuel at an exorbitant rate. The one flight which reached Mach 1.6 ran out of fuel; the pilots bailed out over North Vietnam and were captured.

Aside from running out of fuel, another reason why fighter planes are not flown faster is that pilots have to identify enemy planes visually before firing at them. The theoretical solution has been to install complex electronic systems to identify and target planes that are not yet in sight. These systems work well in one-on-one simulations, but have no reliable way of distinguishing friendly from enemy planes in crowded, chaotic skies. In practice, pilots will probably still prefer to go slow enough and get close enough to see what they are shooting at.

The new electronic systems have been a tremendous success, however, at eating up money. Each F-15 has 45 separate computer circuits which can, and often do, break down and need replacement. Even the computers used in the repair shop to locate the F-15's problems have their own frequent breakdowns, and the Air Force has been unable to recruit and retain enough computer technicians to make the system run smoothly. A 1980 Defense Department memo showed the average F-15 was ready to fly only 56% of the time, and needed 34 hours of maintenance per flight. Another new plane, the F-111D, was ready to fly 34% of the time and required 98 maintenance hours per flight.[16]

Supersonic flight, while it may help, is not a prerequisite for creating such defects. Similar problems have shown up in the Army's new M-1 Abrams tank, costing $2.7 million apiece. Loaded with complex new systems never before installed in a tank, the M-1 appears to have become useless in any actual battle. It has a breakdown requiring 30 minutes or more to fix, on average, every 43 miles. It gets less than 1400 feet to a gallon of gas, so it must be accompanied by a fuel truck. Its transmission is too fragile to allow it to dig itself into fortified positions, as earlier tanks did, so it must also be accompanied by a specialized bulldozer. Its gun wobbles in cold weather, its hydraulic fluid is extremely flammable, its turbine engine is an easier target for heat-seeking missiles than earlier diesel engines, its side, top and rear armor is thinner than on older tanks, and on and on. The M-60 tank which it is replacing did much better by most of these standards, as do current Soviet tanks.[17]

A similar story could be told about other high-priced weapons which our generals like to collect. There is no plausible use for some of the most expensive new toys at the Pentagon, just as there is no real military spending gap, no window of vulnerability threatening our security, and no need for the MX and other agressive advances in nuclear weaponry.

Winning one for the Gipper

Why, then, do we maintain such a massive and costly military establishment? Military Keynesianism is one important reason, but not the whole story. The U.S. is also trying to regain its former power to dominate much of the Third World.

Before the Vietnam War, the U.S. was able to intervene at will in most underdeveloped countries. Alliances, military aid, occasional CIA coups, even visits from the Marines were used to keep friendly governments in power throughout the "Free World." It was not a world of political freedom that we were defending: the rulers of Indonesia, Brazil and other Free World stalwarts, like our allies in El Salvador and Guatemala today, were in the habit of torturing and killing any visible opposition. But it was a world in which multinational corporations were free to come and go as they pleased, an alliance for profits if not always for progress.

Overseas activity has proved profitable indeed for U.S. business. The share of corporate profits coming from foreign investment has mounted steadily since World War II, reaching 24% by 1980.[18] While much of this comes from Europe and Canada. the U.S. corporate stake in the Third World is also substantial. U.S. companies depend on foreign oil and other raw materials, on foreign markets for their exports, and on the growing opportunities to invest in low-wage manufacturing abroad.

In the early 1970s, U.S. control of this economic empire was dealt a disastrous double blow. Defeat in Indochina revealed the limits of military intervention, while the rise of OPEC weakened U.S. control over the most important foreign resource. Saving "our" oil in particular, and our access to Third World economies in general, seemed to require a new strategy.

For a few years the Pentagon and the State Department leaned toward the development of regional policemen, or "subimperial powers," as they were sometimes called. The U.S. would send military aid to Brazil, allowing the Brazilian military to be the guardians of South America. Or, in one of the most important, best-armed cases, massive aid to the Shah of Iran would surely allow him to keep the Middle East under control. . .

The downfall of the Shah in 1979 ended the brief era of reliance on other countries to police the Third World for us. Not that regional allies became irrelevant; U.S. military aid and weapons sales to Turkey, Egypt, Saudi Arabia and Pakistan increased after the "loss" of Iran. But more important was the massive propaganda campaign for a renewed U.S. military buildup. Then, a year later, when the Soviet Union invaded Afghanistan—the kind of event that U.S. right-wingers had spent thirty years breathlessly waiting for—the floodgates of the new militarism were pushed wide open.

So the U.S. has returned to a post-Shah policy remarkably like pre-Vietnam policy. Once again, the best defense is a strong offense: let's win the next one for the Gipper. The invasion of Grenada in 1983 showed that the new militarism was not just talk. Any government that displeases the White House risks being overthrown by the Marines. Even an impoverished island nation of 110,000 people, following World Bank advice to expand its airport and attract more tourists, can be portrayed as an ominous threat to U.S. security, calling for military intervention.

In preparation for more Grenadas to come, several chunks of Reagan's Pentagon budget are aimed at improving our ability to attack Third World countries that displease us. The Rapid Deployment Force is supposed to be able to put 24,000 troops and their weapons in the Persian Gulf area, or almost anywhere else in the world, on two weeks' notice. Its expenses for such items as desert fighting gear and Indian Ocean bases are of little relevance to defending the United States.

The Navy's expansion from 450 to 600 ships, one of Reagan's most expensive plans for the 1980s, is also aimed largely at Third World intervention. The Soviet Union and its allies have almost no warm-water ocean ports. We are far ahead of them in naval tonnage and firepower, and our lead is increasing.

The large size of many of our ships ironically constitutes further evidence that they are intended to intimidate poorly-armed Third World nations. Our biggest ships are so expensive that they can only be used against countries that have no chance of sinking them. Even the Pentagon, with its privileged access to the nation's treasury, cannot afford to have a destroyer (costing up to $1 billion) or a nuclear-powered aircraft carrier ($3.5 billion) sunk by "smart" anti-ship missiles.

These computer-guided naval weapons give a tremendous advantage to the defense. In the Falkland Islands war in 1982, Argentina fired six Exocet missiles, destroying two British ships and badly damaging a third. One of the ships, the H.M.S. Sheffield, cost $50 million; the Exocet missile which sank it cost less than half a million dollars. Similar successes with earlier smart weapons were achieved by both Egypt and Israel in Middle East wars and by India in its 1971 clash with Pakistan.[19]

Our biggest-ticket items of all, the nuclear-powered aircraft carriers, are so immense—the flight deck covers more than four acres—as to present easy targets for attack. (U.S. naval strategists claim that our aircraft carriers, with their accompanying ships and planes, can defend themselves against any attack. But a detailed review of such claims in *Scientific American* recently found ample grounds for skepticism.[20]) Aircraft carriers were developed in an era when ships could not be hit from 20 miles away and more; today carriers must be kept far offshore and far away from enemy ships, or more likely must be used against countries which do not yet have modern anti-ship weapons.

One of the fastest ways to cut the military budget would be to reduce the number of aircraft carriers. Each one taken out of service would save roughly $200 million annually, the operating costs of a carrier and its accompanying ships. In addition, the accompanying ships could be reassigned to other uses, reducing the number of new vessels the Navy plans to build. Instead the Reagan administration has decided to build two more giant carriers, in addition to the 13 we already have. The construction costs alone will be at least $12 billion (for two carriers and accompanying ships) during the 1980s. Meanwhile, computers are getting smaller, cheaper, and more powerful all the time, and it is reasonable to expect that computer-guided anti-ship missiles will do the same. The Exocet, a French missile, was designed in 1972. When carriers number 14 and 15 hit the water in 1991 or thereafter, how far will smart anti-ship weaponry have progressed?

As they say in Washington, throwing money at problems does not always solve them. Our pre-Vietnam ability to control other countries will not be restored at the sight of a fourteenth or fifteenth aircraft carrier. Our overwhelming military superiority did not hasten the return of U.S. hostages from Iran in 1980. Our abundant military aid has not made the government of El Salvador able to win the hearts and minds of its people. Nor are we really likely to invade an oil-producing country and seize its oilfields, a fantasy which reappears during every shortage; a handful of people opposing our invasion could quickly sabotage oil wells and pipelines in ways that would take years to repair.

An occasional intervention, as in Grenada, may remind other countries that we are armed and dangerous. Aiding and financing right-wing attempts to overthrow a popular government, as we have done in Nicaragua, may make some countries think twice about speaking crossly to us. Flexing our military muscle undoubtedly strengthens our hand in some minor conflicts. But that is not the same as being able to win the next Vietnam-style war or to save the next dictator who, like the Shah of Iran, is threatened by his own people.

Unfortunately, it works

The problem with supply-side economics, and often with monetarism, is that they do not work as advertised. Application of these theories does not result in prosperity for large numbers of people. The problem with military Keynesianism, on the other hand, is that it does work. Building aircraft carriers, nuclear weapons, even M-1 tanks, does provide employment. As Keynes himself noted in the 1930s,

> Pyramid-building, earthquakes, even wars may serve to increase wealth, if the education of our statesmen on the principles of the classical economics stands in the way of anything better.

Keynes went on to comment, "It would, indeed, be more sensible to build houses and the like..."[21]

In a technical sense, too, military spending unfortunately works. Despite periodic snafus, on the level of amphibious vehicles that sink, most of our weapons will, if properly aimed and fired, destroy the person (or metropolis) they are pointing at. Millions of people have been taught how to do this; in the wake of Reagan's budget cuts, it is one of the few forms of job training still offered by the federal government. Technological progress, too, is encouraged by the pursuit of ever more exotic and difficult techniques of devastation. The result is not quite as many jobs, or as attractive a form of technological advance, as peaceful alternatives would provide; but in a crude quantitative sense, military spending keeps the economy going.

Thus Reaganomics stands indicted for its successes as much as for its failures. Recognizing, at least implicitly, that government spending is needed to stimulate and direct the economy, the Reagan administration has opted for spending money on threatening nuclear holocaust, rattling sabers and aircraft carriers at the Third World, and permitting colossal levels of waste.

Perhaps the conclusion that military Keynesianism is a success stems from a misstatement of goals. We need not only a policy that will create jobs and incomes, but also some assurance that we, and our children and grandchildren, will survive to enjoy the fruits of prosperity. And with that broader goal in mind, there must be a better way to run an economy.

chapter 6

free
to
lose

*A propaganda campaign would have you believe these
deficits are caused by our so-called massive tax cut and
defense buildup. Well, that's a real dipsy doodle.*
— Ronald Reagan, November 16, 1982

The president often manages to achieve a folksy, down-
home style as he delivers his logical blunders. Call it dipsy doodle
or gospel truth, the fact remains that the federal budget is the
difference between what the government spends and what it
receives in taxes. If you increase military spending and cut taxes,
the deficit is bound to go up—as the Reagan administration has
so ably demonstrated in practice.

But Ronald Reagan wanted to do more than give refund
checks to the rich and second helpings of everything to the
Pentagon. He also wanted to stop inflation. This was the task of
the third major strand of Reaganomics. Behind the siren song of
the supply side and the trumpet call of the new militarism,
another voice could be heard. It was the monotonic drone of
monetarism: hold down the money supply...cut the budget...
ignore the economy's ups and downs..."steady as she goes".
Less flashy and attractive than the other theories, it was the
perfect counterpart to the Republican campaign slogan, "Stay
the course."

Monetarism has a brief, though esoteric, economic policy
argument. The one true path to prosperity is for the Federal

83

Reserve System to maintain a slow, constant growth rate of the nation's money supply for a period of years. Aside from monetary policy, the government should leave the economy alone. The result will be full employment without inflation—someday.

But like other theories, monetarism does not (outside the realm of textbooks) begin with economic technicalities. Monetarism, too, justifies itself in sweeping ideological terms. Not the wild-eyed dreams of supply-side paradise, nor the hysteria over the Soviet threat, but rather the subtler beauties of the untrammeled free market are in this case the selling point for conservative economics.

The founding father and undisputed high priest of monetarism is Milton Friedman. Winner of a Nobel Prize in economics, he has done many technical economic studies, and influenced government leaders including Augusto Pinochet in Chile and Margaret Thatcher in Britain as well as our own Richard Nixon and Ronald Reagan. He has also produced some of the best-known popularizations of conservative economics. In 1980 he and his wife coauthored *Free to Choose*[1], a book dedicated to the proposition that the market is a Good Thing but government is not.

Free to Choose shares many common themes with George Gilder's *Wealth and Poverty* (discussed in Chapter 2): disgust at the concept of publicly provided social services, scorn for concerns about economic equality and justice, and adoration for the miracles wrought by private business decision-making. They differ in the political myths they use to defend capitalism, and in their prescriptions for economic policy. Their differences reflect a debate which has raged within the Reagan administration. And as the defects of supply-side theory became inescapable, the Friedmans' side began to win the debate.

Take the money and run

You can, if you are an egalitarian, estimate what money income would correspond to your concept of equality. If your actual income is higher than that, you can keep that amount and distribute the rest to people who are below that level.[2]

That's just one of the choices open to you in the brave new economic world foreseen by the Friedmans. There's so much you could choose to do, there's so much the economy could do in response to your choices. . . .if only those government bureaucrats would unleash the marketplace and let us be free.

Free to Choose spent months on the bestseller lists in 1980, curiously enough placed on the nonfiction side. It is a highly partisan book: Ronald Reagan raves about it on the jacket flap, while Jimmy Carter and Teddy Kennedy come under attack in the text. Its message, though, is being listened to by Democrats as well as Republicans.

Its message is nothing less than a redefinition of the word "freedom." The market offers freedom: if you want Rice Krispies for breakfast, no one can force you to buy Cheerios instead. Government, in contrast, means coercion: if you want your taxes spent on street repairs but a majority of your neighbors are more concerned about fire protection, your dollars are enslaved and shipped off to the fire department against your will. The book's title and almost every page of the text hammer home the redefined concepts. Buying and selling are freedom; voting and planning are slavery.

The market is not only personally liberating, claim the Friedmans; it also creates the best of all possible economies. In support of this claim they present one big theory and one big distortion of reality. The theory, one of the great insights of the eighteenth century, is the explanation of the way competitive markets work. If consumers suddenly want more tomatoes and less lettuce than before, they will be willing to pay a higher price for tomatoes as they compete for scarce supplies. Lettuce, on the other hand, will go partly unsold unless the price is lowered. Farmers will notice these changes, conclude there's more money to be made in tomatoes and less in lettuce, and adjust next year's crop accordingly. The Friedmans, like Adam Smith before them, find this terribly exciting. You get exactly the right mix of tomatoes and lettuce, with no planning or government regulation required.

The distortion of reality is the assertion that the whole economy can and should work this way. The Friedmans simply announce that the biggest businesses, like small farmers deciding between lettuce and tomato crops, are controlled by consumer choices.

In fact, the people responsible for pollution are consumers, not producers. They create, as it were, a demand for pollution. People who use electricity are responsible for the smoke that comes out of the stacks of the generating plants.[3]

Notice the disappearing trick that is being done here. If the market is so powerful that every detail of a large company's behavior is a response to consumers' wishes, then the very possibility of corporate power has vanished. Since it is continually forced to respond to your choices, big business is on your side.

The chief economic function of a department store, for example, is to monitor quality on our behalf. ... Sears, Roebuck and Montgomery Ward, like department stores, are effective consumer testing and certifying agencies as well as distributors.[4]

Not so with big government. Aside from a few minimal functions such as providing police, military forces and (the Friedmans' favorite) a stable currency, the government should leave everything alone. Social services and programs are inferior to charities, private philanthropy and reliance on your own family.

The difference between Social Security and earlier arrangements is that Social Security is compulsory and impersonal—earlier arrangements were voluntary and personal. Moral responsibility is an individual matter, not a social matter. Children helped their parents out of love or duty. They now contribute to the support of someone else's parents out of compulsion and fear.[5]

Since they believe freedom resides only in the most individual actions, it is not surprising that the Friedmans view moral responsibility the same way. If nothing that anyone wants or needs is produced by the government, if nothing that makes people feel free depends on social interactions with others, then no one has the right to make any claims on you. Why worry about old people, when you can take the money and run?

Having grasped this thread of an essentially anti-social understanding of society, it is not hard for the Friedmans to unravel the justification for most government programs. "The minimum wage law requires employers to discriminate against persons with low skills," the Occupational Safety and Health Administration is "a bureaucratic nightmare that has produced an outpouring of complaints," and on and on.

What's wrong with this picture?

There are major flaws throughout the Friedmans' free market ideal. In brief, they misrepresent the nature of corporations, of people, and of government.

The Friedmans' central claim is that corporations, if freed from government interference, would be forced by the market to do nothing but carry out consumers' desires. This is vegetable-stand economics, a far cry from the reality of power wielded by such giants as Exxon, General Electric and IBM. It is one thing to point out that even the biggest firms must eventually sell their products to someone. It is quite another thing to allege that multi-billion-dollar corporations' decisions about advertising, plant location, labor relations and environmental protection are dictated by the will and whims of consumers.

There is no record of the consumer demand for Hooker Chemical's faulty waste disposal at Love Canal. No Mobil customers have demanded that part of their oil dollars be spent spewing forth propaganda in newspaper ads. Nor have Exxon customers insisted on that company's unsuccessful ventures into the computer and electric motor industries. Telephone users are not responsible for most operators being female and most repair personnel being male; coal users do not clamor for more deaths in the mines. Indeed, both the telephone and coal industries continued to thrive in the 1970s despite federal regulations that began to alleviate sex discrimination and on-the-job accidents. The Friedmans may decline to mention it, but corporate power lives on despite them.

If the Friedmans' corporations are strangely weak, their people are implausibly affluent and self-reliant. Crusading for the belief that freedom means shopping, the Friedmans employ a favorite metaphor of economists: "When you vote daily in the supermarket, you get precisely what you voted for, and so does everyone else." There are at least three problems with the supermarket as polling place.

First, some people may ignore the Friedmans' advice and persist in wanting things that don't fit on the shelves. There is no way for a single individual to freely choose mass transit, pollution control, a ban on nuclear power, clean streets, fire protection, guaranteed incomes for senior citizens or other intrinsically social goods and services. Collective choice and government action are required, once it is admitted that people have legitimate social wants and needs.

Second, unlike some other polling places, one person may arrive in the supermarket with ten times as many votes as another. The richer you are, the more you get to say about what will be produced. The undemocratic implications of "dollar voting" do not seem to trouble the Friedmans. In fact, they offer an aggressive defense of the virtues of income inequality:

> It is certainly not fair that Muhammad Ali should be able to earn millions of dollars in one night. But wouldn't it have been even more unfair to the people who enjoyed watching him if, in the pursuit of some abstract ideal of equality, Muhammad Ali had not been permitted to earn more...than the lowest man on the totem pole could get for a day's unskilled work on the docks?[6]

Third, the Friedmans' marketplace includes the world of work as well as consumption. You are free to go shopping for jobs, too, or for places to invest your idle millions. The following statement is supposed to apply to decisions about taking a job as well as buying a breakfast cereal.

> The key insight of Adam Smith's *Wealth of Nations* is misleadingly simple: if an exchange between two parties is voluntary, it will not take place unless both believe they will benefit from it.[7]

A misleadingly simple insight, indeed. In some exchanges one party is making the voluntary choice to take a minimum-wage job instead of starving, while the other is making the voluntary choice to employ 101 workers instead of 100.

But working people are not a species with whom the Friedmans are particularly familiar. Many readers will be surprised to learn that "you can travel from one end of the industrialized world to the other and almost the only people you will find engaging in backbreaking toil are people who are doing it for sport." In a chapter on unions, the first example to be discussed is the American Medical Association, perhaps a group the Friedmans have more social contact with. One lesson drawn from this "union" is that "physicians are among the most highly paid workers in the United States. That status is not exceptional for persons who have benefited from labor unions." (Actually, in 1979 physicians had an average income of $78,000, while the average production worker made under $22,000 in every major industry, including auto, steel, coal mining and trucking.[8])

Having distorted the economic roles of corporations and people, the Friedmans do the same for government. Big government is not a plague that fell from the sky to afflict a healthy private economy. It is only in part a response to popular pressure for social programs. In many ways big business needs big government. The Pentagon protects multinational corporations around the world, provides jobs and lucrative weapons contracts, and stimulates new technologies such as computers. Highways, fire protection, police and other basic services are necessary to any business. Many regulatory agencies have been "captured" by, and primarily serve the interests of, the industries they are supposed to regulate—as the Friedmans acknowledge. Even social programs may protect business stability by coopting potentially dangerous popular unrest. Such cooptation appeared both politically necessary and economically affordable in the 1960s and early 1970s; by now, it looks expensive and dispensable.

The seductive promise

Strange as they are, the theories in *Free to Choose* have become a force to be reckoned with. Their strength reflects the corresponding weakness of liberalism; the Friedmans at least have a clear, powerful ideal to advocate. In the realm of academic economics, liberals as well as conservatives attempt to impress their students with the theoretical charms of the competitive market. The difference is that liberals are more prone to admit its impossibility and concentrate on empirical description of the economy or debates over minor reforms. Conservatives like the Friedmans prefer to pretend that the reality of big business conforms to their competitive ideals.

In government, the liberal programs and initiatives the Friedmans are attacking really don't work very well. Who, after all, wants to defend the present systems of public education, welfare or Social Security taxes? Rather than reshaping them, though, the Friedmans want to abolish these and many other government functions. Clearly, major changes are needed throughout the government apparatus, but the Friedmans propose to throw the concept of modern plumbing out with the bathwater.

The "abolitionist" approach to government programs has a strong popular appeal. Many people feel powerless today, in the face of both government and corporate bureaucracies. Even the recipients of government services are often frustrated, insulted and demeaned by the manner in which the services are provided. *Free to Choose* offers the spurious but seductive promise that you could indeed have power over the way things are done, if only the government would let you. In the absence of a more sensible route to participation in making society's major decisions, the Friedmans' promise sounds attractive to many.

Doubtless the Friedmans' imagery appeals as well to captains of industry. They should find it gratifying to hear themselves described as obedient servants of the public will. Such emphatic denials of the power of big business can only help capitalists in their public relations and political battles. The attack on social programs also fits well with the current corporate agenda. Cutbacks in public services and benefits will make people more dependent on their employers and less able to resist wage cuts in recessions.

Wage cuts are the key to yet another marvelous feature of the Friedmans' free market mechanism. Unemployment, left to itself, is said to be self-correcting. Workers who are unemployed will offer to work for less, thereby inducing employers to hire more of them. Like vegetable stands with surplus tomatoes, workers will compete in lowering the price of labor until the surplus disappears. Of course the machinery of the market can be gummed up by unions, civil service rules, minimum wage laws, or anything else which inhibits workers from selling themselves more cheaply. The role of the government, then, is to leave the free market alone—and to make sure that everyone else does, too.

But there is one area in which monetarism casts the government in a more active role: in setting monetary policy, that is to say, in controlling the nation's supply of money. Even the most ardent free marketeer will usually acknowledge that the creation of money must be regulated, to maintain public faith in the value of the currency and to keep the wheels of commerce turning. As the name of the theory suggests, monetarists attach great importance to this regulation of money.

Strange but untrue

Monetarist theory asserts that people and businesses spend whatever money they have on hand at a steady rate, called the "velocity of money." The idea is that your money is burning a hole in your pocket; it's got an urge to travel—and to travel at a predictable rate. The velocity of money, roughly speaking the number of times the average dollar changes hands annually, is in simple formulations of monetarism said to be constant from year to year. More subtle recent versions allow the velocity to change, so long as it changes very gradually and predictably. In either version, the speed with which people spend money is said to reflect institutional factors such as the frequency of wage payments and the structure of the banking system, which change slowly if at all.

If the velocity of money is constant, or nearly so, then monetary policy will have powerful effects on the economy. If the government allows the total supply of money to grow more rapidly than the real production of goods and services, spending will also grow faster than production. This means intensified competition for limited supplies of goods and services, leading to price hikes. Therefore, as the Friedmans conclude in *Free to Choose*, "there is only one cure for inflation: a slower rate of increase in the quantity of money." The correct, noninflationary policy is to figure out how fast real production normally grows—a range of 3% to 5% per year is often mentioned—and then be sure that the money supply grows no faster than that.

Such policy prescriptions are only as good as the theory on which they are based. The notion that money has a roughly constant urge to travel is not intuitively very compelling. People at times spend money quickly, at other times save it for a rainy day or a specific future purchase. For the country as a whole, the rapid cultural and economic changes of recent years could easily have upset any past regularities in financial habits.

A theory cannot be rejected, however, just because its assumptions sound weird. In the natural sciences, theories such as quantum mechanics start from extremely counterintuitive assumptions but lead to remarkably accurate predictions. Some important theories, that is, have turned out to be strange but true.

Monetarism, on the other hand, is strange but untrue. It neither starts from a plausible description of behavior, nor does it lead to accurate predictions. Among economists, monetarism has lately been gaining in popularity, as traditional Keynesian policies have failed. Yet at least twice within the last decade, monetarist predictions have completely missed the mark, due to unexpected shifts in the velocity of money.

One such shift occurred in the late 1970s. From 1974 to 1979, the velocity of money increased sharply; predictions based on historical data through 1973 were quite visibly wrong. This episode is by now reasonably well-known, and has even been written up in textbooks.[9] Economists speculated after the fact that rapid innovation in financial markets, including the introduction of NOW accounts and money market funds, had caused the jump in velocity—but no one predicted the jump in advance.

The second episode was more recent, and perhaps more damaging to the theory. For it occurred in 1982, when monetarism was the reigning doctrine of U.S. monetary policy. This time velocity plummeted downward; again, no one really knew why, or predicted the shift in advance. In the words of the February 1983 *Economic Report of the President*, a thoroughly monetarist document,

> The 1982 decline in the velocity of money—as measured by [either of two common statistics]—was historically atypical.... These velocity declines were the largest since 1959, the earliest year for which the Federal Reserve has published data....
>
> The uncertain cause of the recent decline in velocity is characteristic of the problems that the Federal Reserve has encountered in applying the new monetary control procedures....
>
> The Federal Reserve was aware throughout 1981 and 1982 that the relationship between the monetary aggregates and economic activity was in a state of flux, and that future velocity trends were uncertain.[10]

It must be hard to write the obituary for your own favorite theory.

A recession, by any other name....

While monetarism may now be dead as a theory, we have all had to live with its results. From 1979 to 1982 Federal Reserve

Chairman Paul Volcker was publicly committed to a monetarist policy. It is no accident that these were years of unusually high interest rates.

Only a fraction of the money supply consists of dollar bills, coins and the like. More important is the amount of balances in checking accounts. As well as directly controlling the production of currency, the Federal Reserve indirectly controls the expansion of checking account balances. When the Fed tries to apply the Friedman cure for inflation, it holds down the growth of the money supply. For that purpose it employs a number of arcane devices which force private banks to limit their new loans to households and businesses. With loan funds in scarce supply, the interest rate shoots up.

The monetarist prescription thus leads to high interest rates, which discourage borrowing. Less borrowing means fewer purchases of houses, cars, new factories and equipment; therefore less employment making these goods; in a word, recession. Or, as the Friedmans say of their remedy for inflation, "Unpleasant side effects of the cure are unavoidable." Monetarism begins to look suspiciously similar to the conventional anti-inflation policies of the 1970s and earlier, fighting price hikes with unemployment. A new jargon in which to talk about it, a technical muddle about the velocity of money, and a tilt toward monetary rather than fiscal policy, may not change the basic anti-inflation strategy—or make it any more popular.

There is even a connection between the unpopularity of the dominant inflation-fighting approach, and the reliance on monetary policy to carry it out. The principal alternative is fiscal policy, the manipulation of government spending and tax levels. In theory, fiscal policy can also be used to cause a recession and thereby reduce inflation. But it is hard to stick to an unpopular fiscal policy for long. Spending and taxes are debated and voted on by Congress, right out in public view; since members of Congress must frequently run for re-election, they cannot always take stands which outrage their constituents. Moreover, fiscal policy is the arena for other conflicts—the fights about tax cuts and military spending, for example—which sometimes take precedence over the battle against inflation. So an anti-inflationary fiscal policy is difficult to maintain.

In contrast, there are few people who understand or pay attention to monetary policy. There are fewer still who have the power to do anything about it. For the last seventy years our money supply has been in the hands of the Federal Reserve. Somewhat like the Supreme Court, the Fed is intentionally insulated from short-term political pressures. The Fed's seven-member Board of Governors, the people who run the show, are appointed by the President to staggered fourteen-year terms. (The only exception is the Chairman of the Fed, appointed to a four-year term which begins midway through the President's term.)

But unlike the Supreme Court, the Fed has no Constitution which it is bound to interpret. The Fed is free to choose whatever monetary policy it finds appropriate, often choosing to follow the informal consensus which exists in top Wall Street and Washington circles. And that consensus favors fighting inflaton with recession, far more often than an accessible, democratic policy-making body ever could.

Historically, the use of tight money to control inflation is older than Milton Friedman and his monetarist theories. In the nineteenth century, the gold standard played the same role. Money had to be backed by gold, and since little gold was discovered or received from foreign trade in most years, the money supply was forced to grow slowly. The result, then as now, was often economic contraction. In the famous words of William Jennings Bryan, the nation was crucified on a cross of gold.

Today the cross is no longer golden. It is made up instead of green pieces of paper, or even of electronic records of bank balances stored deep in the memory of computers. But the monetarist crucifixion is no less painful—as shown by the experience of governments which have tried to follow Friedman's advice.

How long is enough?

In Chile, General Augusto Pinochet seized power in 1973. Pinochet's military coup killed democratically elected President Salvador Allende and thousands of his followers, and led to widespread "disappearances," tortures and other human rights violations. And the coup brought monetarism to Chile.

Helped from the start by Chilean disciples of Milton Friedman, Pinochet decided in 1975 to get economic advice straight from the horse's mouth. As Friedman recalled his contact with Pinochet in a later interview,

He seemed a perfectly reasonable human being. . . .He asked sensible questions. He was able to understand the answers. I had a very favorable impression of him on that level. We did not talk about any of the political aspects.[11]

Naturally Friedman advised Pinochet to try sharp cuts in government spending, tight limits on the growth of the money supply, and increased freedom for business. The general avidly followed these instructions, and a few years of impressive growth ensued, thanks in part to favorable world market conditions for Chilean copper exports. For a while Chile was described as the monetarist miracle.

But when the world market slumped in the 1980s, the Chilean economy was crushed. The country's GNP fell 14% in 1982; the official unemployment rate hit 20% in 1983. Growing numbers of Chileans defied the military government and took to the streets in protest—and Milton Friedman declared that Chile was not a fair test of his theories.

On the other side of the globe, Margaret Thatcher came to power in Britain by more peaceful means, in 1979. Again Friedman was invited to offer economic advice. Thatcher, determined to stop inflation, embarked on a clearly monetarist course: budget cuts, tight controls on the money supply, and confrontation with the labor movement over wages and work rules. The policies were a preview of Reaganomics, as were the results. British unemployment hit a post-World War II record, basic industries collapsed faster than ever, and social unrest spread through the nation. Only the stratagem of fighting and winning a war with Argentina over some rocks near the South Pole finally restored Thatcher's popularity. Friedman's judgment? "No, of course Britain is not a fair test of monetarism."[12]

Back in the U.S., monetarism made its Washington debut in 1969-70, during the Nixon administration. But after a spell of moderately tight money and a rather small recession failed to make any noticeable dent in inflation, Nixon abruptly reversed himself. In 1971 he declared that he was a Keynesian now, and set about stimulating the economy and experimenting with wage-price controls in order to get himself re-elected. By the time the wage-price controls began to fall apart and inflation again became a problem, in 1973, Nixon was sinking into the morass of Vietnam and Watergate, and was no longer much concerned with the fine points of monetary policy.

Inflation subsided for a while in the economic slump of 1975—and so did government interest in monetarism. The next stab at applying the theory began in 1979, when inflation returned to double-digit levels. President Carter was politically unable to stop inflation via fiscal policy, which would have required drastic tax increases or budget cuts. Instead he appointed Paul Volcker head of the Federal Reserve, with a clear mandate to zap inflation via monetary policy.

Before the Volcker era the Fed had usually tried, with some success, to keep long-term interest rates roughly stable. But in October 1979 Volcker announced that, exactly in line with monetarist theory, the Fed would now pay more attention to slowing the growth of the money supply—even if that led to increases in interest rates. Though it lurched back and forth a bit in the process, the Fed did succeed in clamping down on the money supply. It also succeeded in setting new record highs for interest rates, with the prime rate (paid by the biggest corporate borrowers) topping 20%.

Important as tight money was to Jimmy Carter's anti-inflation efforts, it was all the more so to Ronald Reagan. Thanks to the tax cut and military spending increase, fiscal policy under Reagan tended if anything to increase inflationary pressure. The tax cut gave households and businesses more money to spend; Pentagon budget boosts meant that the government itself was spending more. All this spending would tend to increase employment, and therefore to push the economy toward higher inflation. Cuts in domestic spending (the subject of the next chapter) were not nearly large enough to remove this stimulus to price increases.

So Reagan was wildly stimulating the economy on the one hand, while trying to stop inflation on the other hand. To perform this juggling trick, the inflation-fighting hand had to be squeezing very hard on the money supply. In 1981 Reagan loyalists in the Treasury Department criticized the Fed for not carrying out a tight enough monetary policy. But by 1982, as 20% interest rates gave way to 10% unemployment rates (and to at least temporarily lower inflation), the Reaganites sensed impending trouble. Now they wanted the Fed to ease up, to show some signs of economic recovery before the midterm Congressional elections.

Miraculously enough, in October 1982 Volcker discovered a "technical problem" which required the abandonment of monetarism and a return to slightly lower interest rates. This change fueled the immense stock market rally which began in late 1982, and the far more modest recovery of employment and production which began in early 1983. The recovery, it should be emphasized, resulted from the abandonment of monetarism, not from success in applying it.

While the stock market loved the new, easier monetary policy, Milton Friedman was not amused. To him it only proved that Reagan and Volcker, like Thatcher and Pinochet, were quitters, unwilling to stay the course:

> The experiment of October 1979 has been abandoned.
> It was terrible that it wasn't carried out.... Inflation
> has been broken. The question is, will it stay broken?[13]

Three years of record-breaking unemployment and interest rates, evidently, are nowhere near sufficient for the permanent monetarist cure for inflation. How long is enough? No direct answer is usually offered. One of Friedman's academic articles, though, suggests that it may take twenty years for the economy to complete its adjustment to a sudden change.[14]

But if even a Chilean dictator is politically unable to stay the monetarist course for twenty years, there is little chance that a U.S. president or Federal Reserve chairman will do so either. Academic monetarists like Milton Friedman will remain free to return to their ivory towers, harrumphing that their theories have never been properly tested—even as those very theories play a crucial role in real-world conservative politics.

As ideology, monetarism recycles the old myth that freedom is achieved only through the marketplace, and that the wishes of consumers command the details of business behavior. (And its popularity must be traced to such political questions. As a predictive science, monetarism is a dud, losing its bet that the velocity of money can be relied on and known in advance.) As policy, monetarism leads circuitously back to the old strategy of fighting inflation with recession. The advantage of the monetarist approach is that, more than other government policies, it is shielded from democratic control—thereby allowing bankers and bureaucrats to decide when it is time to sacrifice a few million jobs in exchange for temporarily slower inflation.

chapter 7

from
cradle
to
grave

Governments can err, Presidents do make mistakes, but the immortal Dante tells us that Divine Justice weighs the sins of the cold-blooded and the sins of the warm-hearted on different scales. Better the occasional faults of a Government that lives in a spirit of charity than the consistent omissions of a Government frozen in the ice of its own indifference.

—Franklin D. Roosevelt, 1936[1]

If indifference is ice, Washington was covered by a glacier in 1981. The White House has offered cradle-to-grave callousness, with proposals ranging from slashing nutritional aid for pregnant women and infants, through stingier funding for terminally ill cancer patients.[2] Between those extremes, there are millions of people who have been iced out of federal programs. People like Danny Salb.

A teenager in a welfare family in Connecticut, Danny had been angry and frustrated in eighth grade. "I was flunking everything," he recalled. Then he got a part-time CETA (Comprehensive Employment and Training Act) job at a dog pound, fell in love with the animals, and decided to study to become a veterinarian. After a few weeks, a teacher noted, "Danny felt better about himself." His grades improved, and he used the money he earned to buy clothes and to help with the family groceries.

In the fall of 1981, as Danny Salb was beginning ninth grade, he and more than 300,000 other CETA employees were laid off by Ronald Reagan. "I was pretty upset," said Danny. He had counted on his paychecks to buy shoes he needed for the winter.[3]

CETA was the 1970s version of public works, the government's admission that jobs had to be created for some of the people who could not find work in the private sector. At its peak in 1977-78 CETA's main public service employment program funded three-quarters of a million jobs, enough to knock most of a percentage point off the unemployment rate. By the end of the Carter administration CETA had shrunk to half that size; in Reagan's first budget CETA was abolished.

> None of us really understands what's going on with all these numbers...we were doing that whole budget-cutting exercise so frenetically. In other words, you were juggling details, pushing people, and going from one session to another, trying to cut housing programs here and rural electric there, and we were doing it so fast, we didn't know where we were ending up for sure....
>
> —David Stockman

Despite the air of frenzied slashing in every direction, a definite pattern can be seen in Reagan's budget cuts. Of the ten major categories of federal spending shown in Table 3, the first five have never been seriously cut. These five areas absorb the bulk of the budget—74% in 1981 and 80% in Reagan's proposals for 1984.

The favored categories include the military, of course, where spending has been growing by about 15% per year. Reagan wants to spend almost a quarter-trillion dollars in 1984; Congressional Democrats may hold out for a hair less. But only the last few percentage points of the growth rate remain open to discussion.

The second "safe" category of the budget is a collection of smaller programs: foreign affairs, space and science, law enforcement, and general government administration. Much of the foreign aid and space programs are closely related to the military.

Interest on the national debt, the third item in Table 3, has been growing almost as fast as the Pentagon budget. Interest payments have been driven up both by Reagan's huge deficits, which increase the amount of borrowing needed, and by Volcker's high interest rates, which raise the cost of borrowing.

Table 3: The Federal Budget, 1981—1984

	1981 actual	1983 estimated	1984 proposed
TOTAL FEDERAL SPENDING	**654***	**805**	**848**
Subtotal: Programs Facing Few Cuts	**481**	**609**	**675**
1. Military	160	215	245
2. Aid, space, miscellaneous (foreign affairs, space, science, law enforcement, administration)	27	31	33
3. Interest on national debt	69	89	103
4. Retirement benefits (Social Security, Medicare, federal employee pensions, other retirement)	202	250	268
5. Veterans benefits	23	24	26
Subtotal: Programs Under Attack	**190**	**216**	**195**
6. Unemployment (unemployment compensation, job training, public works jobs)	29	43	34
7. Social welfare (food stamps, welfare, Medicaid, housing aid, other social services)	76	84	83
8. Agriculture	6	21	12
9. Economic development (transportation, energy, commerce, community development, revenue-sharing)	64*	54	53
10. Education	15	14	13
Undistributed receipts**	-16	-20	-23

Notes: All figures are fiscal year (October 1-September 30) outlay totals, in billions of dollars.

*Government budget figures include the cost of the strategic petroleum reserve in 1981, but exclude it in later years. Here it is excluded in all years, lowering the usual 1981 figures by $3 billion.

**Some minor sources of funds are always listed this way, as "negative expenditures" in the budget. The largest undistributed receipts are income from Outer Continental Shelf oil and gas wells.

Source: Budget of the United States Government, fiscal years 1983 and 1984.

Funding for retirement programs is largely secure, but not as a result of White House generosity. Most of Reagan's proposed cuts in Social Security and Medicare were quickly defeated by angry mobilizations of senior citizens (and others who expect to be senior citizens someday). The 1983 Social Security financial "reform" did include some benefit cuts, and minor attacks continue on the fringes of Medicare and federal employees pensions. But for the most part the battle to save retirement programs appears to have been won. (For more on these programs, see the next chapter.)

The last of the relatively safe areas is veterans' benefits, long a politically untouchable program. The Reaganites have done little more than small-scale sniping at the veterans' cost-of-living increases. Slow growth in the cost of this program reflects the declining number of eligible veterans.

These five categories absorb the lion's share of all federal tax dollars—but have suffered fairly few of the Reagan cutbacks. Instead, the administration's target has been the remaining areas of the budget, a small and shrinking share of federal spending.

Attacking employment programs, the Reagan administration has ended CETA, and slashed the Jobs Corps and other training services. It has also made life harder for those who are receiving jobless benefits. Among the casualties of the budget wars were trade adjustment assistance (extra-long benefits formerly paid to those thrown out of work by imports); unemployment benefits for people leaving the armed forces (now only half as long as civilian benefits, encouraging re-enlistment); and the automatic extension of benefits from 26 to 39 weeks in a recession (formerly available nationwide). In the latter area the Reaganites introduced a complex state-by-state formula for determining where extended benefits would be granted. The formula was intricate and bizarre enough to deny unemployment benefits even to Michigan, with its depression-level joblessness, for three months in 1981-82.[4] Congress, however, eventually wearied of such statistical nonsense, and insisted on re-enacting a broader program of extended benefits nationwide.

Stories of cutbacks may seem hard to square with the overall budget figures. As shown in Table 3, federal spending related to unemployment (including unemployment compensation, job training and CETA programs) leaped up from $29 billion in 1981, the last pre-Reagan budget, to $43 billion in 1983. This leap, though, was almost exactly matched by the jump in the number of people unemployed.

The number of people officially counted as unemployed—those who are not only out of work, but also have actively looked for a job within the last month—was 8.0 million during the 1981 budget year. But the budget estimates in Table 3 assume 11.8 million unemployed people in 1983, and 11.3 million in 1984.[5] When unemployment rises there is an automatic increase in federal spending, both for unemployment benefits and for most social welfare programs. People who lose jobs often become eligible for food stamps, housing aid, and so on. (The population which needs and receives benefits from these programs is larger than the officially unemployed; it includes many who work at very low-wage jobs, cannot work, or have given up looking for jobs. But changes in the official unemployment rate are a good approximate measure of changes in the need for social services.)

So, one might ask, how does social spending compare with the level of unemployment? Table 4 answers this question. It is the result of dividing budget figures, like those in Table 3, by the number of officially unemployed people in each year.

Table 4: Unemployment and Social Welfare Programs Spending Per Unemployed Person, 1981-1984

	1981	1983	1984
Unemployment programs	3.6	3.6	3.0
Aid to Families with Dependent Children	1.1	0.7	0.7
Food stamps and nutrition programs	2.0	1.5	1.4
Housing assistance	0.9	0.8	1.0
Medicaid	2.1	1.6	1.8
Other health and social services	3.4	2.5	2.5
TOTAL	13.1	10.8	10.4

Notes: All figures are in thousands of dollars per unemployed person. "Unemployment programs" here is the same category as in Table 3. The other items here add up to the social welfare category in Table 3. "Other health and social services" includes all health programs other than Medicare and Medicaid, welfare programs other than AFDC, and miscellaneous services.

Unemployment spending per jobless person was unchanged from 1981 to 1983, while the cost of living rose about 10%.

Corrected for inflation, then, unemployment spending per person actually fell 10%. For 1984, the Reaganites proposed a much sharper cut. A new round of finagling with the formulas was to yield both a reduction in the fraction of the unemployed population eligible for benefits, and a lower average benefit for those who do qualify.[6]

Welfare fraud

The most-maligned public program has been called on to make even greater sacrifices. Yet, popular stereotypes to the contrary, it is hard to solve very many economic problems at the expense of welfare. The entire array of social welfare programs accounted for less than 12% of the federal budget in 1981, and less than 10% in Reagan's proposals for 1984. Aid to Families with Dependent Children, the very heart of the dark imagery of welfare extravagance, is under 1% of federal spending. Looking at Table 4, it is hard to find any programs which are experiencing runaway costs: under Reagan it is the number of people in need which has grown uncontrollably, not the spending per needy person.

Ronald Reagan is not the first politician to perpetrate the fraud that welfare is becoming too expensive for the nation to afford. He has, however, acted on this misconception with particular ruthlessness. For conservatives like Reagan, cracking down on welfare, nickel-and-diming the women and children who depend on AFDC, has an ideological importance far transcending its paltry budgetary savings.

Newly restrictive rules have been adopted, aiming at cutting benefits and throwing people off welfare entirely. Under the old rules, welfare recipients who began to work lost their benefits only gradually as their incomes rose, to provide incentives for welfare mothers to get jobs. Under the Reagan rules benefits are lost much more quickly, as Kathleen Devlin found out.

Living in Massachusetts with her two children, Devlin was on AFDC until October 1981. Then, having just started work as a bank teller, she was informed that her $500 monthly take-home pay made her ineligible for AFDC under the new federal rules. But due to a bureaucratic error her welfare checks of almost $400 a month continued to arrive through the following January. She repeatedly asked her local welfare office if she was really entitled to the money; getting no definitive answer, she continued to cash and spend the checks. In February the state welfare department discovered its error and threatened to sue Devlin to recover the $1500 it had incorrectly sent her. "I have no money and no bank account," she said. "And they want to take me to court. They make the mistake and they can still get the money back."[7]

Kathleen Devlin got only about $100 a month more for going to work than she did for staying home on welfare. Under the old rules her increase in income would have been at least twice as great, since she still would have qualified for partial AFDC benefits. Her case is not unusual.

Before the Reagan budget took effect, more than one out of every four women on welfare already held a paying job, but one that paid so poorly that the woman was still eligible for AFDC. The cutbacks have fallen most heavily on this group, often called the "near-poor,'since they are not quite as destitute as those who are entirely dependent on welfare. The near poor, it seems, mut be inspired to work harder by having their welfare checcks cut. Clearly, they are a different breed from the near-rich, who can be inspired to save and invest only by lavish tax breaks.

But as the carrot of monetary incentives to get off welfare is shrinking, the stick is getting bigger. To make sure that welfare recipients are visibly suffering for their checks, workfare programs are now required in all states. In one variant, the "jobs club," recipients are forced to put in 40 hours a week reading want ads, making telephone inquiries, writing resumes, and going for interviews. This leads, if anywhere at all, to low-wage, dead-end, high-turnover positions—short-order cook, telephone salesperson, typist. Recipients are required to take the first job offer they get, regardless of location, pay, or child care availability.

A second form of workfare requires recipients to work off their welfare grants in unpaid jobs, at a rate close to or equal to the minimum wage. The more children a welfare mother has, the larger her grant, and the more hours she must put in. Only women with children under six are exempted (in some states, only women with children under two).

Neither the jobs club nor the forced-labor style of workfare offers child care and job training, which might enable recipients to enter long-term employment. In any of its forms, workfare is nothing more than a politically acceptable method of harassing welfare recipients. It places almost no one in paying jobs, and it saves the taxpayers insignificant sums of money. Its significance, rather, is its message to others, a message straight out of George Gilder: stay off of welfare! Women should stay with men who can support them, no matter how abusive the relationships; people who are employed should stay where they are, no matter how oppressive the jobs. After all, consider the alternative—consider being on workfare.

But the worst may be yet to come. In California, the state where Reaganomics was born, a new method of saving money on welfare has been invented: the nineteenth-century poorhouse. To receive general assistance in Sacramento County, you must live in a dormitory, do menial work for the county three days a week, and spend the rest of your time job-hunting. Even married couples are separated into men's and women's dormitories, and everyone must be present for a 9 PM roll call each night. In the morning there is oatmeal, dry toast, and exactly one cup of coffee per person. According to a member of the staff, "we cannot afford to give everyone more than one cup."[8]

Thus the cult of taking from those who have the least, the endless pursuit of supposed welfare fraud, leads ultimately back to the era of Charles Dickens. Excited by the success of workfare for AFDC, the Reagan administration wants to apply similar rules to food stamp recipients. Is the Sacramento County poorhouse the ghost of Christmas future for us all?

Grapes of wrath

Men who can graft the trees and make the seed fertile and big can find no way to let the hungry people eat their produce. Men who have created new fruits in the world cannot create a system whereby their fruits may be eaten. And the failure hangs over the State like a great sorrow. The works of the roots, of the vines, of the trees, must be destroyed to keep up the price, and this is the saddest, bitterest thing of all.

—John Steinbeck[9]

The Grapes of Wrath, the classic saga of hunger and resistance in the Great Depression, sounds less like ancient history than it did a few years ago. Under the Reagan administration, small farms are again going broke and being foreclosed in record numbers. The federal government is buying mountains of surplus food, and paying farmers to grow less. And this at a time when food stamps, school lunches and other programs that feed hungry people are being slashed.

Thanks to Reagan's cutbacks, more Americans go to bed hungry every night. During the 1970s the expansion of food stamps, school lunches, nutrition aid for pregnant women, infants and children (WIC), and other programs had nearly eliminated serious malnutrition in this country. But to the Reaganites, the growth of these programs was a sure sign of waste, and a top target for budget cuts. Documenting the waste involved, the President did point out in a news conference that someone was once seen buying a bottle of vodka with food stamps in Chicago. (Not, of course, that there is any across-the-board hostility to federal financing of liquor: mixed into a Bloody Mary and served with a business lunch, vodka is tax-deductible.)

To stop such sinful excesses among the poor, the administration has made food stamps much harder to get. The first Reagan budget lowered the eligibility ceiling for a family of four from $14,000 to $11,000. Each successive budget has made food stamp regulations tighter, benefit levels lower, and total funding leaner. The WIC program, faced with repeated death threats from the White House, has been kept alive each time by Congressional supporters; its funding, however, has failed to keep up with inflation and growing numbers of people in need.

In the school lunch program, the proposed nutritional insight that ketchup is a vegetable was laughed out of court, with the result that subsidized lunches must continue to include real vegetables. The less humorous cuts in eligibility for the program, and in the funding for subsidized lunches, survived. In 1982 alone, 3.2 million children and 2,700 schools dropped out of the school lunch program.[10]

Overall, the cutbacks can be measured by the figures in Table 4: food stamp and nutrition funding, per person in need, has been declining sharply. The impact of the cutbacks can also be described in less statistical terms: "It's hard to watch kids starve, but that's what we do," said Dr. Jennifer Rathbun of Boston's Children's Hospital. "There's no question we are seeing more children with malnutrition [in 1982] than we saw a year ago."[11]

In much of the world, hunger and malnutrition reflect the absolute lack of food. The problem in the United States is just the opposite. In the early 1980s several years of bumper crops coincided with the worldwide economic slump, which lowered both exports and domestic sales of U.S. farm products. This led to immense surpluses of most crops, and to rising government expenses to buy up the surplus in order to support farm prices. By 1983 government spending on price supports had soared to at least $21 billion, an amount almost equal to the net income (after expenses) of all the nation's farms. That is, without price supports farmers as a group would have been flat broke, averaging about zero take-home pay for the year.[12] One of the success stories of free enterprise in good years, agriculture is completely dependent on public support and planning in bad times.

The Reagan administration has continually tried to lower or abolish many of the farm price supports, and to cut costs through reorganization of the programs. Congress, however, seems to be sentimentally attached to the survival of farming as an occupation, and has defeated most of the cuts. As seen in Table 3, the administration still optimistically forecasts much lower spending for 1984—an event which is not likely unless demand for farm products revives.

Saving farmers from economic collapse is a worthwhile endeavor. But that is not to say that it is presently done in a sensible or equitable manner. Most programs pay in proportion to production or acreage, giving the most to the largest, wealthiest farms. A limit of $50,000 per farmer, attached to some programs, was removed in Reagan's proposals for 1984.[13] Small farmers, on the other hand, may not receive enough to save them from bankruptcy, particularly if they have to repay money borrowed at the high interest rates of recent years.

Moreover, the pattern of supports results from the clout of different farms groups, not from a thought-out policy. Dairy farmers have done better in Congress than grain producers, which is why the government buys so much surplus cheese and butter—the two commodities occasionally given away to the poor. While other government agencies try to discourage smoking for health reasons, the Department of Agriculture in effect bought nearly one-third of the tobacco grown in 1982, generously encouraging the production of this deadly crop.[14]

And above all, the embarrassingly unprofitable abundance of our farms remains locked in warehouses. It rarely reaches the soup kitchens where the urban poor line up in the long winters of

Reaganomics. Today no less than in the 1930s, surplus food that cannot be fed to the hungry is, in Steinbeck's words, the failure that topples all our success.

Chopping through the net

There are more social services and more tragedies in the same vein. Congress has often resisted the worst of the Reaganites' desires, but has still tolerated sharp reductions in benefit levels. Housing assistance, which subsidizes the dwellings of nearly ten million people, is repeatedly scheduled for demolition. According to Republican Senator John Tower, "The Administration wants a heavy emphasis on the private marketplace and is not terribly interested in public housing."[15] Medicaid, the system of health care for the poor, is slowly being dissected just as millions of unemployed workers are losing their health coverage. The result is that the ancient diseases of poverty reappear: at Chicago's Cook County Hospital there were 600 admissions for tuberculosis in 1982, double the level a year earlier.[16]

In every area of social services, the picture is clear. The "truly needy," for whom Ronald Reagan periodically professes concern, are in fact the biggest losers in the Great Budget Upheaval of the early 1980s. White House rhetoric talks of preserving the "essential safety net" of services for the poor; actually the administration has been chopping through the net as fast as Congress will allow. While Reaganomics is building a more perfect warfare state, it is also dismantling what there was of a welfare state.

For its most ardent supporters, this was the point all along. The right wing, new or old, has always been hostile to the notion of income redistribution and benefits for the poor. Reagan's budget cuts are a key to solving inflation the conservative way, by driving down the wages, the working conditions and the bargaining strength of those at the bottom of the working class—those most dependent on government benefits for survival. Laid-off workers, deprived of unemployment checks, food stamps or welfare, will be forced to take any sweatshop job in sight. Once at work, they will find any proposed pay cut or speed-up to be an offer they can't refuse. Wages will fall, profits will rise, price stability and economic growth will return. Someday the prosperity may even trickle down to those whose involuntary sacrifices made it possible.

Other budget cuts, less directly related to driving down wages, still reflect similar right-wing prejudices. Throughout the broad areas of federal spending for education and economic development (see Table 3), Reaganomics proclaims that small is beautiful.

In education, spending on school desegregation is down; programs for the disadvantaged and the handicapped have come under fire, though Congress has so far defended them. Middle-income families have been hurt by cuts in student loans and other funds for higher education. "Thank God my parents got divorced," exclaimed Holly Koch, a student at the University of Hartford in Connecticut. The first year of Reaganomics took away $500 of her work-study grant, while her college costs rose $1500. If her parents had still been married, she would have lost even more under the new aid formula. As it was, she was forced to work longer hours during the school year, while taking a full load of courses. If she was starting over, she said, she would start at a community college to save money.[17]

Transportation spending is increasing only for airports and (to a lesser extent) for highways. Funding for mass transit and railroads is being cut. Will this create a financial crisis in metropolitan areas which depend on public transportation? Of course—that is precisely the point. To quote the droll phrasing of Reagan's 1984 proposal for mass transit, "Shifting financial responsibility to local authorities should make low-cost alternatives more attractive."[18]

In the Department of Energy, all non-nuclear research, conservation programs and energy regulation are receiving lower funding every year; only nuclear research is thriving. In the Department of the Interior, national parks, forests, pollution controls, sewer systems and other programs are having their allowances reduced. Budget cuts are helping to starve out regulatory agencies, speeding the task of deregulation.

Still, it seems, waste is in the eye of the beholder. While slashing away at the basic services and programs once provided by the government, the Reagan administration has not changed the opulent lifestyle taken for granted at the very top of the federal bureaucracy—a world in which merely flying first class is peanuts. J. Lynn Helms, head of the Federal Aviation Administration under Reagan, took government executive jets rather than commercial flights for all business travel in his first eight months in office. The cost to the taxpayers was a mere $417,000; airline tickets for the same flights would have cost less than

$13,000. And a general insisted on taking a C-140 Air Force transport rather than a smaller T-39 plane to get himself from Washington D.C. to a base in Nebraska, saying he needed the extra speed. The larger plane saved him 15 minutes; the additional cost was $12,400 for that one flight.[19]

Robin Hood in reverse

With luck, many of Reagan's proposed budget cuts may never become law. Fun though it was demolishing useful government activities the first few times around, there are signs that the fascination is fading. Popular and Congressional resistance to further cuts in the same programs has been steadily stiffening. Reagan got most of the cuts he asked for in his first year, but no more than a third of the amount requested in his second year, and likely even less thereafter.[20] Still, the services and programs destroyed by the early rounds of Reaganomics have not, for the most part, been rebuilt.

What has been accomplished by all this devastation? First and foremost, the poor have been made poorer. With less generous benefits, the unemployed have been made more desperate to get back to work, no matter how low the wages. Those unfortunate enough to depend on welfare have been made more visibly miserable than ever. And the nation has been disabused of the silly notion that surplus food should be shared with the hungry.

Second, education and economic development programs are also in worse shape than they used to be. States and cities have been forced to take over some functions once funded by Washington, causing tax increases in many areas. This also hurts the poor, since state and local taxes are more regressive (that is, they fall more heavily on lower incomes) than federal taxes. But the gap left by Reagan's cutbacks has not been entirely filled by local funds; there is simply less being done in education and economic development.

Finally, the savings have been eaten up by Reagan's increases in other parts of the budget. There is no official calculation of how much has been cut overall. However, a rough estimate is easy to produce. If there had been no cuts, then total spending on education and economic development might have kept up with inflation from 1981 to 1984. Likewise, spending on unemployment and social welfare, per unemployed person, might have kept up with inflation. In that case, 1984 federal spending would have been $86 billion higher than Reagan's proposals. That is, if all the proposed cuts for 1984 were adopted, the total cuts for Reagan's first three budgets would be $86 billion.

This did not mean, though, that the taxpayers saved $86 billion. The increase in interest payments on the national debt, and the increase (beyond inflation) in the Pentagon budget from 1981 to 1984 swallowed $78 billion, or almost all of the savings from civilian cutbacks. The Reagan administration has been playing Robin Hood in reverse, taking funds from the poor and the inner cities to give to the military and the wealthy bondowners who receive the interest on the national debt.

chapter 8

lost
in
the
reshuffle

*My administration seeks to limit the size, intrusiveness,
and cost of Federal activities as much as possible
...ways are being found to streamline Federal activity,
to limit it to those areas and responsibilities that are
truly Federal in nature...and to aid State and local
governments in carrying out their appropriate public
responsibilities....*
—from Ronald Reagan's 1984 Budget Message

Beyond the specifics of each year's proposed budget cuts lies
a larger philosophical issue. Is big government getting too big?
Should many functions of government be returned to smaller
units, to states or cities, closer to the people they serve? Can
reorganization make public services better and cheaper, without
hurting those who depend on the services?

With questions like these, the Reagan administration has
struck a responsive chord in many people. The federal government does seem immense, out of control, remote from those it
serves. Undoubtedly some kinds of reorganization could make it
better.

But there is a right way and a wrong way to set about
reshaping the government. The wrong way is unfortunately illus-
trated by the Reagan proposals for block grants and for the "New
Federalism." The right way is, in part, suggested by the workings
of the Social Security system, and by the experience of other
countries.

The new federalism: no strings, no funds

Amid great fanfare about states' rights and decentralization, Reagan has sought to turn many federal programs over to state and local governments. Many formerly separate programs have been consolidated into a few block grants to states and localities; more programs are proposed for inclusion in block grants each year. The block grants come with no strings attached—and with distinctly lower funding, sometimes 25% lower, than the programs had before consolidation.

Reactions from state and local officials have been overwhelmingly negative. The cuts in funding that go with the new block grants have not escaped anyone's attention. "The situation is dismal," said Wilson Riles, then California's superintendent of public education. "We have more freedom, yes, that's true. But it is almost exclusively the freedom to make the agonizing choices of where to cut."[1]

At first glance the cuts in funding may appear to be the only drawbacks of the block grant approach. Many of the old programs did not work very well; part of Reagan's rhetoric about cutting through red tape and allowing greater local control sounds appealing to anyone who has tangled with federal agencies in the past. But beneath the rhetoric, the switch to block grants conceals some sweeping political changes.

Many of the now-consolidated programs were created in the 1960s and early 1970s, in response to the demands of the civil rights, Black Power and welfare rights movements. The legislation creating the programs often reflected (to be sure, in a limited and distorted fashion) the politics of the times. Affirmative action requirements, funds earmarked for particular low-income groups, community monitoring or feedback on programs—all such stipulations may get lost in the reshuffle as Reagan reorganizes social services.

Local control of block grants therefore means that groups formerly protected by law are now pitted against each other in the struggle for shares of a smaller pie. In the harsher climate of the 1980s, minorities and disadvantaged groups find it much harder to win their battles over again. How much of the education block grant will be spent on bilingual and special needs programs, and how much on advanced computer courses preparing the fastest students for their careers in Tomorrowland?

The same process would be taken much farther by Reagan's New Federalism. In its first incarnation, the plan called for

Washington to give the states full responsibility for AFDC, food stamps, mass transit funding, and many other programs. To finance these programs, the states were to get the revenues from federal alcohol, telephone and tobacco taxes, and half the federal gasoline tax and crude oil windfall profits tax. At first these taxes were to be collected by the federal government and turned over to the states; later the taxes were to be abolished at the national level, leaving states free to set tax and benefit levels themselves.

The response from state officials, Republicans and Democrats alike, was chilly. Most of the revenues included in the deal came from the windfall profits tax, which only a handful of oil-producing states could possibly collect, and from the gasoline tax, which would be most valuable to rural states (which have the most driving, and gasoline consumption, per capita). For New York, according to former governor Hugh Carey, the costs of the new federalism package would have been nine times as large as the revenues it offered.[2] Faced with such arithmetic, the original plan was soon dead.

But the idea rose from its ashes. New Federalism II, proposed in 1983, offered to give states a different set of programs and an unspecified set of federal revenues to finance them with. State and local officials seemed no more interested in the new plan. John Gunther, executive director of the U.S. Conference of Mayors, asked, "Why is it that this Administration, which says it wants to make things easier for local governments, keeps telling us what we want or need?"[3]

Even if it included only taxes that were equally accessible to all states, any new federalism scheme would be biased toward elimination of the programs involved. States and cities already compete in offering tax breaks to lure corporate investment and jobs away from each other. A plan that let states decide whether to impose taxes and provide benefits would allow the stingiest states to up the ante in the poker game of bidding for business. What state could dare to keep taxes high enough to finance food stamps, at the cost of losing a computer company to its neighbor? It is precisely in order to avoid this debasing spectable that social services, and the taxes that support them, should remain the responsibility of the federal government. Many aspects of administration and control of federal programs might well be decentralized—but to avoid regional competition, tax and benefit levels should be kept uniform throughout the country.

Coming of age

Even the newer "new federalism" proposal has, for the time being, been dropped. It appears that this was not the way to restructure the federal government. A better approach can be found by examining another budget battle, one in which Reagan was largely defeated: the proposed cuts in Social Security and other retirement programs. Among federal programs, the system of retirement benefits is uniquely and unmistakably popular, as the budget-cutters found out. If the goal is truly to make the government serve the people, perhaps Social Security should be taken as a model for other services.

What is different about Social Security? No other program is so nearly universal. It sends benefit checks to 36 million people, and accounts for 38% of the income received by the 65-and-older population. (Other government pensions provide another 8%, and public assistance 2%; in all, a total of 48% of all elderly income comes from the government.)[4] Its benefit formulas are relatively simple, widely understood, and widely perceived as equitable. Because of its simplicity, it can be administered with fairly little overhead (for a federal program). While it is by far the largest civilian program in terms of spending, it is far from the worst in terms of public image of unresponsive bureaucracy.

In particular, Social Security is more popular than the array of "means-tested" programs such as welfare, food stamps and public housing, for which you must prove that you are sufficiently poor or otherwise unfortunate enough to receive benefits. The notion of means-tested programs seems to make sense in the abstract: why waste scarce resources providing benefits for those who are already well off? In practice, however, the process of testing eligibility forces the government to make intrusive and inevitably somewhat arbitrary judgments about the details of peoples' lives. Worse yet, means-tested programs in an environment of scarce resources will normally be underfunded, forcing extremely low eligibility cutoffs. Providing support only to the utterly desperate, such programs are a natural focus of resentment for the near-desperate, who pay taxes but just miss qualifying for benefits.

By contrast, there is no one who is resentful because of just missing eligibility for Social Security. It is accepted because it is seen as a right to which everyone is entitled, not a privilege of those who claim (justly or unjustly) to be worse off than average.

Other programs, then, might do better if they became more universal: socialized medicine instead of Medicaid and other health programs; family allowances instead of welfare; food stamps or free food available to the bulk of the population.

The problem is that while this sounds attractive, it also sounds expensive. Indeed, it has been widely claimed that Social Security has been on the edge of bankruptcy, saved only by the benefit cuts and tax increases voted in 1983; Medicare (health coverage for senior citizens, administered through Social Security) is said to be facing a similar crisis in the next few years. Less, not more, in the way of universal services appears to be on the agenda.

Yet this gloomy outlook is not justified by the facts. A closer look at the workings of Social Security shows that it is well within our means to preserve and expand this popular area of universal services.

Just like the rest of us

Dismal forecasts about Social Security and Medicare financing can be made in part because of the needlessly complex way in which these programs are financed. When you and your employer make payments to Social Security, the money is divided among three trust funds, for retirement, disability and hospitalization. Then when you retire, become disabled, or qualify for Medicare benefits, your check is paid by the appropriate trust fund. The fact that they are called trust funds, and the natural sequence of first paying in, then getting money out later, seem to suggest that your payments have been saved and then paid back to you. Actually, this has never been the case. The funds maintain only a small balance, often under a year's worth of benefits. Your payments now finance today's retirees; your retirement benefits later will be drawn from the taxes paid in by the people who are working at the time.

This "pay-as-you-go" approach had the advantage of allowing the system to start up almost immediately. The first Social Security legislation was passed in 1935, and the first benefit check was paid in 1940. The more cautious approach of saving each worker's contributions and then paying them back in benefits would have required waiting much longer, perhaps for decades, before beginning substantial payments. But "pay-as-you-go" financing runs into trouble in two situations: either when the country is suffering from inflation and unemployment, or when the elderly population grows faster than the number of employed workers.

In the short run, Social Security finances have looked bad lately because too little has been paid into the trust funds, and too much paid out. There is nothing mysterious about this; you may have noticed the same problem in your own checkbook, for example. Moreover, Social Security's troubles have the same causes as many people's financial woes: unemployment and inflation. Unemployment lowers tax collections; no one pays Social Security taxes when they are out of work. Inflation, on the other hand, raises benefit costs—both because benefit checks are adjusted to keep up with inflation, and because Medicare costs keep rising. The high unemployment and inflation of the last ten years or so, in other words, have caused the immediate crunch on Social Security funding.

One implication of this is that the exact surplus or deficit in the trust funds at some time in the future cannot be projected with any certainty. You can make the numbers better or worse by varying your forecasts about inflation and unemployment. Back in 1977 the Carter administration proudly predicted that Social Security finances were secure for several decades—assuming that inflation would stay under 5% annually. In 1981 the reported problems of Social Security abruptly got worse—because official forecasts were now based on the assumption of double-digit inflation and 9% unemployment.[5]

With a bad enough depression Social Security might go bankrupt, along with the rest of us. Using more moderate forecasts, the 1983 changes will solve the short-run problems. The largest immediate changes were the six-month delay in cost-of-living increases for retirees, and the acceleration of the scheduled 1985 and 1990 tax increases to 1984 and 1988, respectively. Other changes include making 50% of the benefits paid to high-income retirees subject to income tax (formerly all benefits were tax-free), ending the tax break for self-employed people, and making all employees of nonprofit organizations, and all new federal employees, subject to Social Security tax. Even under fairly pessimistic assumptions, these measures will generate enough revenue to get through the 1980s.[6]

A dependent by any other name

The longer-run problems are more serious. In the fuzzy area of long-run forecasting, the decisive factor is the number of people expected to retire each year. Social Security finances should look better from now to 2010 because the relatively small groups born between 1920 and 1945 will be retiring. After 2010 the much larger population born in the post-World War II baby boom will be retiring. At that point the ratio of people receiving benefits to people paying taxes into the trust funds will start to soar (unless there is another baby boom in the next decade, producing a surge of new workers by around 2010). By 2030 or so, many projections show Social Security, under its present system of financing, in serious trouble.

The 1983 changes in Social Security financing aimed to address this problem, too. In addition to the short-run changes, Congress boosted the age at which full retirement benefits can be received to 66 for those born in 1943 or after, and to 67 for those born in 1960 or after. Official forcasts now show that the 1983 changes, combined with a good bit of luck and very little inflation (4% a year) would solve the long-run problem.[7] If, however, the average rate of inflation is above 4%, or if anything else works out worse than the official forecasts assume, the Social Security crisis will return with a vengeance early in the next century.

When that happens, are lower benefits or later retirement ages inevitable? How much security can we afford for the senior citizens of the year 2030 (i.e. everyone reading this book in the 1980s who is still alive by then)? Whatever financing system is used, retired people are ultimately being fed and clothed by the labor of those who are currently working. But retired people are not the only ones in that position. Children are dependent on current workers in exactly the same way. So, too, are those working-age adults who, voluntarily or involuntarily, are out of work.

The costs of young and old dependents may even be similar: a West German study found the cost of raising a child to age 20 to be one-third to one-fourth greater than the cost of supporting the average 60-year-old for the rest of his or her lifetime.[8] Suppose, then, that we consider dependents of all ages as placing roughly equal burdens on the working population, and ask the broader questions: How many dependents per worker can we afford? How many will we have in the dreaded years beyond 2010?

Remarkably, it turns out that the standard Census Bureau projections of population trends imply that there will be fewer dependents per worker in the next century than there were from 1950 to 1970. The figures are shown in Table 5.[9] The table is based on the assumptions of a slight improvement in life expectancies, a "zero population growth" birth rate, no net immigration, and continuation of the 1979 pattern that the number of workers is about three-quarters the number of people aged 18-64.[10]

Using these assumptions, we are headed toward a society with 1.34 dependents per worker—four dependents for every three workers, if you dislike fractional people. In 1960, when the baby boom generation was born but not yet working, there were 1.65 dependents per worker, or five for every three workers. Projecting the population decades into the future is an iffy business, of course. Nonetheless, the Census Bureau's best available guesses imply that the anticipated crisis in Social Security 30-50 years from now does not reflect any overall increase in the burden

Table 5: Workers and Dependents, 1950-2050 and Beyond

	Percentage of Total Population That Is:				Dependents Per Worker
	0-17	65+	18-64	Working	
1950	31.0%	8.1%	60.9%	39.8%	1.51
1960	35.7	9.2	55.1	37.8	1.65
1970	34.0	9.8	56.2	39.9	1.51
1979	28.4	11.2	60.4	44.9	1.23
2000	26.1	12.7	61.2	45.5	1.20
2025	24.0	18.2	57.8	43.0	1.33
2050	23.8	18.5	57.7	42.9	1.33
Long-Run Limit	23.4	19.0	57.6	42.8	1.34

Notes: The first three columns are based on actual Census data for 1950-1979, and on Census Bureau Series II-X projections for the future (see text for description of the underlying assumptions). Any society which maintains a zero population growth birth rate tends towards a stationary age distribution; that distribution, for the Series II-X assumptions, is shown here as the long-run limit. The fourth column, for 1950-1979, is civilian employment plus Armed Forces employment as a percentage of total population of all ages. For the future, the 1979 ratio of people working to people 18-64 years old is assumed to continue. The final column is simply calculated from the fourth column: dependents per worker is the reciprocal of the fraction of the population that is working, minus one.
Source: *Statistical Abstract of the United States, 1980*, p. 30-31, and *Economic Report of the President, 1981*, p. 264.

of dependents on the working population. If we could afford to live through the childhood of the baby boom generation, we can afford to live through its retirement.

The problem is that even if the overall burden is not increasing, the mix is changing. The dependent population used to include relatively more children and fewer senior citizens than it will in the future. There is no existing mechanism that smoothly transfers resources once spent on children—the public funds for education, and the private expenditures for diapers, bicycles and all the rest—into programs such as Social Security.

Raising the retirement age, the "long-run" solution adopted in 1983, certainly reduces Social Security costs: it forces each of us to work and pay taxes a little longer, and to collect benefits for a little less of our lives. If the funding crisis reappears in decades to come, it could of course be solved by raising the retirement age still further—why stop at 67? But the advocates of later retirement, generally economists and politicians, are not themselves engaged in physically demanding occupations. Among blue-collar workers and others in stressful jobs, early retirement is very popular. At General Motors, after the United Auto Workers won a good pension plan, the average age at retirement dropped from 70 in 1950 to 58 in the late 1970s.[11]

A more humane approach would seek voluntary ways of getting more people to work. (Strange as it may seem at a time of high unemployment, the long-run economic problem of Social Security is one of finding more workers to support all those retirees.) In Sweden, for just this reason, employers are required to offer employees in their late 50s or 60s the option of reduced hours of work at the same hourly pay rate. This makes it possible for many more people to choose to keep working, rather than seek early retirement.

Even more could be done: new jobs could be created, often for less than 40 hours a week, specifically for older workers. To cite one important example, some people in their 60s and 70s would make good childcare workers, enjoying a chance to be "foster grandparents"—and expanded childcare opportunities would free some younger parents to go to work, raising the number of people working and paying taxes still further.

There is a long-term problem in financing Social Security retirement benefits. If it is not addressed, this most popular, most universal public service will be progressively undermined in decades to come. In view of the gradual aging of the population, what is needed is a transfer of some of the funds formerly spent on childrearing to the support of senior citizens, and a reshaping of employment to accomodate older workers. With such changes, our system of retirement benefits can be made secure for the twenty-first century.

The high price of health

The second major area financed through Social Security taxes is Medicare, which covers most health care for retired and disabled people. Here the funding problems are even more severe, and were not addressed by the 1983 changes. Trouble is in store for Medicare not only because of the growing number of retirees after 2010, but also because of the continual escalation of health costs.

The U.S. now spends over one-tenth of its gross national product on health care, more than any other country. Yet the results are dismal: the infant mortality rate, for instance, is higher here than in Hong Kong and Singapore, as well as at least a dozen European countries.[12]

In this case, universal services—a national health care system, or "socialized medicine"—would probably save money. A complete public takeover of health care would allow cost-cutting in two major ways. First, straight salaries instead of fee-for-service payments would eliminate the present incentives for doctors and hospitals to order needlessly complex tests, equipment and operations. (A recent study in the *New England Journal of Medicine* found that profit-making hospital chains, one of the fastest-growing sectors of the health industry, are profitable not because of lower costs or greater efficiencies, but because they do more complex, expensive procedures per patient than non-profit hospitals.[13])

Second, a unified system of free or nominal-fee health care for all would eliminate layer upon layer of bureaucracy and paperwork currently required to prove someone is financially eligible for treatment. Vast bureaucracies already administer most health care: government programs pay for two-fifths of all medical care; government and health insurance companies between them pay for two-thirds.[14] A single health care administration which did not have to keep records of patients' financial status could make health care less, not more, bureaucratic.

The notion that such changes could lead to big savings is not a guess about an untried utopia. In this country pre-paid group health plans are one of the cheapest forms of medical coverage; a national health system would in a sense be one big pre-paid group health plan. In other countries, nationalized health systems exist in Canada and throughout Europe, in fact in every other industrial nation except South Africa, with impressive results. Under their union contract, auto workers receive the same medical benefits in Canada as in the U.S.; in Canada those benefits cost roughly half as much.[15]

Iron lungs and steel hearts

Few voices in the current debates about Medicare advocate moving toward national health care. The more common direction is to propose cutbacks, to make Medicare more expensive, more restricted, perhaps even to convert it to a means-test program like Medicaid, the program of health care for the poor. What lies down this road can be seen in the sorry state of disability insurance, the smallest and most politically vulnerable of the Social Security family of programs.

To qualify for disability benefits, you must have been working for half of the last ten years, and must have a disability which has kept you from working for the last five months, and will keep you jobless for the next twelve months or more. However, the disability need not be caused by work. Three million people are now receiving benefits. Blacks are more likely to be disabled than whites; in either race, the most frequent recipients are older, poorly educated men.

After the present form of the disability program was created in 1960, costs rose rapidly. Ever-growing numbers of people qualified, and payments were climbing by more than 8% annually for most of the 1960s and early 1970s. One could conclude from this that astonishing, and perhaps growing, numbers of people are disabled. However, the more popular interpretation in Washington was that people were cheating, and that it was time for a crackdown.

As in many other programs, cutbacks began in the final years of the Carter administration, then were made much worse under Reagan. Many new applications were rejected, and existing cases were reviewed and thrown off disability, all with more attention to costs than to people's health. Horror stories inevita-

bly appeared, as steel-hearted administrators threw people off
the disability rolls; at one point, a man in an iron lung was
declared fit for work and ineligible for benefits.

After publicity about this and other extreme cases, the
administration decided that examiners must physically see each
recipient before stopping their checks. Perhaps the most gro-
teque errors are now being prevented. Still, people are being
thrown off disability so arbitrarily that, in New York at least, half
of those who appeal win reinstatement; for those who contact a
legal aid lawyer before appealing, the proportion rises to almost
four-fifths.[16]

Again, there are more reasonable alternatives. A better
approach would focus on understanding and preventing the
sources of disability. Though disabilities need not be work-
related, they often are. West Virginia routinely has one of the
highest rates of disability in the nation; in 1976, before the
cutbacks began, it had 7 disability recipients for every 100
workers.[17] This is at least a strong hint that coal mining in
particular is a hazardous occupation. More money spent on mine
health and safety might bring big payoffs in reduced disability
costs.

The other states with the highest disability rates are all in the
Southeast. The explanation is less obvious, but could include
lack of preventive health care for blacks and low-income whites,
farm-related accidents, or industrial accidents and illnesses
related to lax government regulation and the absence of union
protection in the area. While disability is a serious problem in all
parts of the country, it does have wide variations in frequency by
state as well as by age, race and sex—all of which should make it
easier to isolate its causes. Then we could save money by preventing future disabilities, rather than by harassing past victims.

In disability, as in other areas, changes are required to make
humane, universal services affordable. If the goal is to reshape
the government to meet our needs, then we cannot continue to
allow millions to be disabled, we cannot tolerate an uncontrolled,
profit-seeking health industry, we cannot ignore the aging of the
population. Preserving and extending the popular areas of universal services now provided by Social Security will force many
changes upon us, some of which will even save the taxpayers
money—but in a different way than the Reagan budget-cutters
propose, by reducing needs rather than cutting off those in need.

chapter 9

zapping labor

*We should look very closely at whether (unions) should
not be bound, as business is, by the anti-trust laws.
Labor has become so powerful and, bargaining on an
industry-wide basis as they do, I've thought for some
time they should be subject to the same restraints that
are imposed on industry and business.*
—Ronald Reagan, April 23, 1980

At times the President lacks the courage of his worst
convictions. So far there have been no White House moves to use
the anti-trust laws to attack unions. But while wrong, as so often,
about the details, Reagan was right about the general approach.
A frontal assault on the power of organized labor is definitely a
part of his economic program.

This is no isolated insensitivity to the interests of a particular
group of workers. It is crucial to the grand design of Reaganomics,
as important to the administration as slashing welfare and food
stamps. The goal is to cure inflation and boost profits at the same
time; the strategy for reaching that goal is to drive down wages
and worsen working conditions, for those at the top as well as the
bottom of the working class. At the bottom, harassing people off
welfare, and slashing food stamps, Medicaid and other services,
increases the number of people desperate to find jobs. Sweatshop
employers are free to choose from a larger pool of willing
workers.

At the top of the working class, meanwhile, the economic slump has driven many people out of their former "good jobs." Part of the contraction may be permanent; many workers laid off in autos, steel and other heavy industries may never be called back to their old jobs. Cuts in unemployment benefits pressure the jobless to give up, to seek lower-paying jobs rather than waiting for their previous employers to recover. For those who remain on the job, Reaganomics has created a climate in which one strong union after another must give back its past gains. Just in case anyone missed the point, the administration went out of its way to pick a fight with unionized public employees as well.

The result is a violent worsening of the best wages and working conditions that labor has been able to achieve. In the 1970s a Nixon aide said that the purpose of wage-price controls was to "zap labor"; in the 1980s the politicians and the policies have changed, but the purpose remains the same.

Naturally, conservative economics has a much prettier way of describing what it is doing to workers. Theories of either the Friedman or the Gilder variety claim that a market economy, left to itself, will automatically achieve full employment. The lower the wage level, the more labor employers will find it profitable to hire. So if wages are free to fluctuate—if there are no union contracts, civil service rules, minimum wage laws or other interferences with the labor market—wages will always reach a level at which everyone has a job. If there is a surplus of labor at today's wage rate, if the number of people wanting work exceeds the number employers can profitably hire, then tomorrow's wage rate will be a little lower. Employers will then find it profitable to mop up the surplus labor, and everyone will live happily ever after.

This is, once again, the economics of the roadside vegetable stand. If prices are free to fall, there can be no such thing as surplus tomatoes. Rather than let them rot, a vegetable stand will cut the price of tomatoes down to the level at which they will all be purchased. In the conservative theory of employment, the only difference is that you are the tomato. And, if Reaganomics has ensured that you have no other choices, you'd work for a lower wage rather than staying home and rotting, wouldn't you?

A number of objections can be raised to the tomato theory of the labor market. First, there is no guarantee that the free market wage level will be high enough for anyone to live on. Some useful items have a free market price of roughly zero—consider zucchini in September, or kittens anytime. In a depression, might labor fall into the same category?

Second, even from a business point of view, low wages are good when companies are looking for employees, but bad when they are looking for customers. This is a fundamental dilemma of a market economy: all businesses want to pay low wages, but sell at high prices to well-paid customers. An across-the-board reduction in wages would lower consumer spending; depending on how pessimistically businesses react to this lower spending, it might lead to a downward spiral into depression, rather than to more hiring. In the nineteenth century, when wages were set by a much more nearly free market than today, there were several panics and depressions in which wages, prices, profits and employment all fell at once.

Third, the free market imagery misrepresents the nature of work in a modern industrial enterprise. Successive tomato sales are brief, isolated acts; the price can be run up or down frequently with minimal damage to buyers or sellers. In contrast, the workers employed by a corporation are engaged in a long-term, interdependent process, in which the results are crucially dependent on the workers' motivation, sense of fairness and security, and willingness to cooperate with each other and train new employees. This social fabric of work would be torn to shreds by constant fluctuations in wages. Long-term stable patterns of wages and seniority-based rules for promotions or layoffs, contrary to the free market theory, are important to the smooth functioning of real-world businesses.[1]

Thus the magic of the marketplace is not enough for employment policy. The conservative theory ignores the need for government action to maintain adequate income levels and prevent depressions. It also overlooks the reasons why, in good times, employers like the dependable labor relations produced by union contracts or similar work rules. Instead, conservative theory is a capitalist tool for hard times, a weapon to be used when business believes that it must break the normal rules and force labor costs rapidly downward to restore profitability.

For in times like the early 1980s, even some of the biggest, unionized corporations have tried to make their workers see themselves as surplus tomatoes whose price must fall. Few companies were harder hit by the economic slump than International Harvester: the markets for its heavy trucks, farm equipment and construction machinery were flattened. Moreover, the company's finances had been weakened by management mistakes, notably by a confrontational attitude toward labor that led to a six-month strike and loss of sales in 1979, the last good year for Harvester's products.

By early 1982 the company was on the brink of bankruptcy. Among other cost-cutting moves, International Harvester decided to close one of its two U.S. truck assembly plants. But rather than saying which one would go, the company announced in July that it was studying whether to close the Fort Wayne, Indiana or the Springfield, Ohio facility. To outsiders, it may have sounded like an innocent, factual statement.

To the workers and communities involved, it sounded more like the opening bell of an auction. In both Springfield and Fort Wayne, city and state officials scurried to assemble packages of loans and guarantees to the company. Workers offered wage concessions, against the advice of their union, the United Automobile Workers. The mayor of Fort Wayne led his city in prayer vigils to sway Harvester's decision. Divine intervention was not forthcoming, however, as the company announced in late September that it was keeping the Springfield, Ohio plant open.

As the company noted in its September statement, "offers of economic assistance in behalf of both communities were so nearly equal that this did not provide an edge to either plant location." Both cities bid about $50 million (or more than $20,000 per job, for the 2200 jobs at stake). The decisive factor apparently was that the Springfield plant was 15 years old, while the Fort Wayne one was nearly 60—information which was no secret before the bidding began. But by claiming that the issue had to be studied further, Harvester won $50 million in concessions from the city of Springfield, the state of Ohio, and the workers at the plant.[2]

The next year, Springfield won another distinction. It was featured in *Newsweek's* 50th anniversary issue as the typical American city of the last half-century. Though scarcely mentioned by *Newsweek*, Springfield's struggle to save its jobs is all too typical of what Reaganomics has meant for labor.

Nothing to say?

For the unions, the signals of bad news to come began almost immediately after the 1980 election, with Reagan's choice of his Secretary of Labor. In past administrations from either party, it had been traditional to pick a labor secretary who was on speaking terms with at least some elements of union leadership—in the hopes of keeping open some channels of communication. Reagan, however, picked an obscure, anti-labor businessman, apparently giving him the job as a reward for his efforts in the 1980 campaign.

Labor Secretary Raymond Donovan was formerly vice-president of Schiavone Construction, a medium-sized company in New Jersey. Schiavone turns out to have a checkered history: in the late 1970s it averaged ten citations a year from OSHA (the Labor Department's Occupational Safety and Health Administration) for "serious" safety violations involving "a substantial probability that death or serious physical harm could result." Schiavone was also plagued by allegations that it had, with Donovan's knowledge, engaged in kickbacks to corrupt union officials and in payments to Mafia-related firms for jobs that were never performed. After a lengthy federal investigation, during which two key witnesses were killed in what the media calls "gangland-style slayings" just before testifying, Schiavone and Donovan were officially acquitted of any wrongdoing.

At the time of his appointment, Donovan was unknown to most national labor and business groups alike. More prominent nominees had been proposed by the Teamsters, the only large union to back Reagan in 1980, and by a number of business organizations. Donovan had been a top Reagan fundraiser, though, and head of the 1980 campaign for New Jersey. Nor was he unknown in the world of far-right, anti-labor zealots: the National Right to Work Committee (a leading anti-union lobby) immediately hailed his appointment, for example.[3]

Other Labor Department officials are cut from the same cloth. OSHA director Thorne Auchter was vice-president of a Florida construction company which was cited for 48 OSHA violation in the 1970s.[4] Auchter was also active in the Reagan campaign in Florida. But the lack of ability to communicate with labor which these gentlemen display may not matter much to the Reagan administration. There is no point in keeping channels of communication open unless you have something civil to say.

Driving down the auto workers

The economic crisis that unfolded in the 1970s was catching up with even the strongest sections of organized labor by the beginning of the 1980s. After a decade of little growth in many industries, energy price explosions, mounting competition from imports, and spiralling inflation, few unions were prospering. Reagan's economic policies proceeded to make a bad situation worse, as the severe recession of 1981-82 led to massive layoffs and an epidemic of management demands for contract concessions.

Until recently the United Auto Workers was a perfect example of a powerful labor organization, just as the auto industry was a cornerstone of national prosperity. In 1978 new records were set for motor vehicle employment and production: one million workers made just over 13 million cars, trucks and buses, and many of the parts for those vehicles. But by 1980 both employment and production had dropped to about two-thirds of those record levels, and stayed that low for more than two years. With the major companies losing billions of dollars, with jobs vanishing almost daily, the UAW was driven into one setback after another: first, lower wages at Chrysler in 1980; then local work rule concessions at many plants; finally, cuts in wages and benefits at Ford and General Motors in 1982. (In return the highest-seniority workers won improved job security, an issue of obviously growing concern.)

The cause of this catastrophe was that suddenly no one wanted the giant cars that Detroit had so profitably produced for decades. Recession and high interest rates lowered auto sales, and the second oil crisis, in 1979, sent those who could still afford cars scrambling after small, fuel-efficient models—many of them made in Japan. The imports were sometimes cheaper than similar domestic models, but that was scarcely the issue. Foreign companies had more small cars available, and had developed a reputation for superior quality that kept them in demand.

U.S. auto companies should have seen that the crunch was coming. They had suffered through two costly warnings earlier in the decade: the first big wave of Toyotas and Datsuns, arriving around 1970, and then the panicked switch to smaller cars after the oil crisis of 1973-74. But auto executives were slow to abandon their traditional big-car orientation. Later, even when they tried, they were unable to keep up with the flip-flops of oil prices and consumer preferences.

From 1975 to early 1979, prices at the gas pump rose more slowly than the general rate of inflation, and sometimes even fell. This stopped all movement toward small car production in the U.S.: consumers were once again willing to buy gas-guzzling big cars, and sales of vans and pickup trucks boomed. The industry invested billions outfitting its plants to produce bigger vehicles, an investment which became worthless when the next oil crisis and small car panic struck, in 1979. Then, just as the expensive transition to small car production got underway, the oil glut depressed gasoline prices, and the few people still buying cars drifted back toward bigger models. Was it really possible for Detroit to make the wrong cars every year?

So the auto slump was no simple result of high wages. It reflected the facts of recession, high interest rates, bad corporate planning, and erratic oil prices. Much has been made of the lower Japanese costs in small car production; a study by Harbour and Associates, a business consulting firm, found that more than half of the Japanese cost advantage was due to better management techniques, in areas such as inventory management and quality control. Only one-fourth of the cost difference was due to lower Japanese labor costs.[5]

Yet U.S. auto workers have been called on to solve the industry's problems by accepting wage cuts. Before the 1982 concessions Ford and GM were paying labor costs of $20 an hour—$12 in wages and $8 in benefits. Constant repetition of the $20 figure in the newsmedia has created the widespread impression that auto workers were uniquely affluent, and could well afford a wage cut to make U.S. industry stronger.

The $20 labor cost was a real cost paid by the companies, which did put them at a real competitive disadvantage. Much of it, though, consisted of costs which did not make the workers feel particularly affluent. One large chunk of hourly benefits is the cost of pension payments and medical insurance for retired UAW members. The total retirement cost is divided by the number of hours of work currently being done, to arrive at a cost per hour. When the industry is depressed, the fixed retirement costs are spread over a smaller number of hours, boosting the hourly cost of benefits. If U.S. auto plants were running full blast like their competitors in Japan, thereby spreading the retirement costs over more hours of work, the $8 hourly cost of benefits might be reduced by as much as $2.

Another factor inflating benefits is the high cost of U.S. health care. General Motors has at times advertised the fact that it spends more on health insurance than on steel. The company seems less eager to point out that under Canada's nationalized health care system, the same medical benefits cost half as much— about $1 an hour less.[6]

Auto workers, in other words, have never felt like they were receiving $20 an hour. Wages of $12 an hour before taxes, while better than most workers' paychecks, do not make you exactly rich. Still, the pressure for auto workers to accept lower wages and benefits proved irresistible. But in the year following the concessions, no stunning upturn in auto company fortunes could be seen. A slow recovery in the industry began only when interest rates eased and customers returned to the showrooms. Like supply-side tax cuts, union concessions are no substitute for a growing economy in which consumers have money to spend.

Watching the sun set

For the building trades, the decline started even earlier than for the UAW. In construction, the end of the post-World War II economic boom brought on a long period of stagnation. As noted in Chapter 1, the value of new construction (corrected for inflation) grew rapidly before 1965, but slowed to an average of only 0.5% annual growth from 1965 to its peak in 1978. The growth that did take place after 1965 was almost entirely in single-family housing, the area in which the building trades unions have always been weakest. All other private construction remained about constant, and government construction was cut back sharply. New highways and schools were no longer being built at the old rates, and nothing came along to replace them.

The stagnation of large-scale construction in the 1970s led to efforts by employers to escape the unions' jurisdiction. Non-union companies sprang up, in many cases created as subsidiaries of unionized firms. The share of nonresidential construction done by union members dropped sharply. Even the one bright spot for much of the 1970s, housing construction, took a plunge in 1979 when Jimmy Carter's efforts to control inflation sent mortgage rates soaring.

Reaganomics has offered more of the same. Budget cuts have curtailed civilian government building projects even more, while there have been only slight increases in military construction. Interest rates have stayed high enough, and consumer incomes low enough, to keep housing starts down. Even in the limited recovery of 1983, interest rates remained higher, and construction slower, than in the 1970s.

The rest of industrial America is on the rocks for related reasons. In steel, autos and construction are normally the two biggest customers. There is immense worldwide excess capacity, and many other countries' steel mills are more modern and efficient, thanks to the U.S. failure to keep up with the latest foreign technologies in the 1950s and 1960s.[7]

U.S. Steel, the nation's largest producer (and among the most technologically sluggish in the past) has spent years closing steel mills and pleading poverty. Yet it was able to borrow more than $6 billion in 1982—not to modernize steel production, but to buy Marathon Oil. If nothing else, it was a move made with exquisitely bad timing. Just as the company entered the oil business, the glut sent oil prices and profits sinking downwards.

The same flair for timing was shown again a year later. After lengthy negotiations, the steel companies finally overcame rank-and-file union resistance and won major wage concessions from the United Steelworkers of America in early 1983. Most steel workers believed the cuts were necessary to remain competitive with foreign steel. Only days after the agreement, U.S. Steel announced that it would begin massive imports of unfinished steel from Britain, eliminating 1000 to 3000 jobs in the U.S.[8]

Trucking lines felt the slump because their leading customers, auto and steel companies, were shipping so much less; their other customers were weakened by the recession as well. The Teamsters were hurt not only by the slowdown in trucking, but also by the 1979 deregulation, which attracted a flurry of new, non-union firms to the industry—some of them newly-formed subsidiaries of old, unionized companies.

Under these pressures the Teamsters' Master Freight Agreement, covering 300,000 truck drivers and warehouse workers, was renegotiated in 1982. The union settled for no wage increase except a limited cost of living adjustment, and allowed changes in work rules that could lead to lower employment—in exchange for improved seniority safeguards for laid-off workers and a promise that unionized companies will stop establishing non-union subsidiaries.[9] Like the UAW settlement with the Big Three automakers, the Master Freight Agreement used to be of great importance in setting a pattern for other union contracts. For the early 1980s, the message these former pace-setters sent to other unions was hardly an encouraging one.

> Rank-and-file rejection of concessions, even at companies that are clearly in trouble, suggests that the level of economic education is not as high as it might be. But this may merely be another reflection of the old adversary relations in the workplace and the treatment of workers as having nothing more to contribute than their hourly labor.
> —*Business Week*, June 14, 1982

Union concessions have been made in many different industries. Electrical workers, rubber workers, meatpackers and others have accepted no wage increases, or even wage reductions, in exchange for explicit or implicit promises of job security.[10] But as *Business Week* observed, such "givebacks" have often faced stiff rank-and-file opposition. The 1982 concessions at General Motors were approved only by a 52%-48% vote among the workers. In steel, top union officials signed three separate wage-cutting agreements with management in 1982-83 before getting one they could sell to the union membership. And in light of U.S. Steel's later behavior, it is hard to say whether the "level of economic education" was higher among those who did believe concessions would save jobs, or those who didn't.

The battles over concessions also show that "the old adversary relations in the workplace" are far from dead. Among other places, class warfare is alive and well in Nebraska. The Iowa Beef Processors plant in Dakota City was the site of a long, bitter strike in 1982, featuring old-fashioned violent clashes between strikebreakers and strikers. Management called in the state police to disperse the strikers with clubs and tear gas. The strike was not about whether the company was in trouble and needed labor concessions; the union had agreed to a two-year wage freeze before the strike began. The company, however, was holding out for a *four-year* wage freeze. At the cost of a four-month strike, the company won.[11]

The White House has no plan for ending the decimation of unions and the decline of once-healthy industries. Indeed, according to the irrepressible David Stockman, this is the plan. As he told the U.S. Chamber of Commerce in 1982,

> High interest rates, unacceptable levels of current unemployment, the lost output we experienced last quarter and this quarter, the financial strains and the rising bankruptcies in the economy, and huge budget deficits that we are coping with—none of these are pleasant facts of life.
>
> But they are all a piece of the same cloth. They are all part of the cure, not the problem. They are all a prelude to recovery, not evidence that the policies should be changed in some fundamental way.

The economic woes of the recession, said Stockman, were necessary evils that would help "end the curse of inflation once and for all."[12]

In other words, the Reagan plan for heavy industry is to watch the sun set over the Midwest. The choice is one with long-run costs to the country: as plants are scrapped, as experienced workers drift away, the old industries become less and less able to expand production in the future. But with those who remain on their old jobs beaten into submission, with those seeking work elsewhere having suitably subdued expectations, business may enjoy a period of little or no growth in labor costs. From the standpoint of Stockman's Chamber of Commerce audience (the particular businessmen who were going broke, of course, excepted) that undoubtedly looked like a great way to fight inflation.

Flying the unfriendly skies

A second area of labor movement strength has been the public employee unions. Government at all levels employs 16 million civilians, about one out of every six workers. (Contrary to the stereotype of swollen Washington bureaucracy, less than one-fifth of public workers are employed by the federal government. Three-fifths work for local governments, and more than one-fifth for states.) At least five million of these public employees are unionized: two million in the two principal teachers unions, one million in the American Federation of State, County and Municipal Employees (AFSCME), half a million in the postal workers unions, and many others. During the 1970s, while industrial unions experienced very little growth, the public employee unions boomed. From 1968 to 1978 AFSCME membership tripled, and the teachers unions doubled.[13]

These unions were bound to be weaker in the 1980s due to the spreading budget crises and cutbacks. One of the past sources of union strength was the fact of secure, growing employment throughout the government. But local tax revolts followed by Reaganomics have reversed this trend. After more than 30 years of growth, public employment reached an all-time high in 1980, and has been declining since then. The layoffs, like the jobs, are primarily in local government, though cuts in federal and state aid to localities are often responsible.[14]

Ronald Reagan has also sent public workers a more explicit message. If industrial unions have gotten a cold shoulder from the White House, government employees have received a knife in the back. The first victim of the administration's assault was the Professional Air Traffic Controllers Organization (PATCO), one of the few unions to endorse Reagan in 1980. Back in October 1980, candidate Reagan wrote to PATCO President Robert Poli,

> I pledge to you that my administration will work very closely with you to bring about a spirit of cooperation between the President and the air traffic controllers.

Less than a year later, in August 1981, President Reagan fired PATCO's membership en masse for daring to strike.

Though the ending was all Reagan's, the beginnings of the PATCO strike stretch back almost a decade earlier. The Federal Aviation Administration, the agency that employs the air controllers, realized in the early 1970s that it had a morale problem in the control towers. Consultants hired by the FAA to study the problem blamed outdated, harsh management methods, and recommended that a "program be undertaken with joint union-management cooperation to improve work life." The FAA, instead, began planning to combat a strike.

The job of air traffic control is a very tense one. It involves long hours of staring at a radar screen and issuing orders to make sure that none of the blips come too close together. It has been compared to playing a "Space Invaders" video game, with the difference that if you let two dots on the screen collide, you lose a lot more than your quarter.

Working conditions had been getting worse in the years leading up to the strike. Air traffic increased 20% from 1978 to

1981, while the number of controllers and the level of control tower equipment remained the same.

The job takes its toll on the workers' health and personal lives: controllers have above-average rates of ulcers, alcoholism, divorce and other problems traceable to stress. Only 11% last to retirement age, despite an easy retirement policy. Half the people leaving the job do so for medical reasons.

PATCO endorsed Reagan in 1980, in fact, out of hostility to Carter's FAA chief, Langhorn Bond, the man the controllers viewed as responsible for the speed-up of their work. Little did they know that Reagan would continue the hated Carter-Bond policies, with two new twists. First, Reagan decided to answer a strike with immediate firings, rather than a warning that firings were imminent. Second, in the weeks just before the strike, Reagan's men at the FAA worked out a plan for reduction in flights that helped the major airlines cut costs. PATCO was unaware of this, and expected that pressure from the airlines would help force a rapid settlement.

By the time of the PATCO strike the airline industry was in need of help from someone. Its problems were due in part to the 1979-80 rise in fuel prices, and in part to the 1978 deregulation of the airlines. Freed of FAA controls over routes and rates and inexperienced at "free market" competition, the airlines overextended themselves. Many new routes were added without cutting out less profitable old ones. By 1981 most planes were flying with more than half their seats empty, and the industry as a whole was losing money.

For the PATCO strike, the FAA required a 25% reduction in traffic at each airport, and more at the busiest airports at rush hours. But the airlines were free to apportion the cutbacks as they saw fit. This gave the airlines a federal mandate to drop their least profitable routes, to scrap their oldest planes, and to lay off some employees—all the while blaming it on PATCO. Under the FAA controls, no new lines could start up, and the extra cutbacks at big airports at rush hours fell much more heavily on the new cut-rate carriers (which specialized in flying only the busiest routes) than on the older, larger airlines.[15]

The airports were in turmoil for months after the strike, but that was not the point. At considerable cost to the nation's air transportation system (and to 11,000 fired controllers), Ronald Reagan made his feelings about public employees perfectly clear:

if you strike, don't expect to come back. The message was not lost on other unions. Postal workers, voting on a contract soon after the PATCO strike, accepted it overwhelmingly; many had intended to strike until they saw what happened to the controllers.

Now the good news

Reaganomics would be a classic "good news/bad news" joke, except for the fact that it is not very funny. The bad news has filled many pages here, and could go on for many more. The good news is, inflation has slowed down.

Any recession slows the rate of price increases somewhat. The 1975 slump, the worst postwar recession until the 1980s, stopped the double-digit inflation of 1973-74, and allowed a brief period of something like price stability in 1976. (Except for economists, no one remembers this today, since the ensuing recovery in the late 1970s soon brought back double-digit infla-tion.) Is the Reagan answer to inflation anything different, or just a little more of the same?

In fact, the two latest episodes of price control via unem-ployment, in the mid-1970s and in the early 1980s, bear many similarities. The gory statistical details of the comparison are presented in Table 6.

Overall, the two slumps knocked similar amounts off the rate of inflation. As seen in the first line of Table 6, the consumer price index slowed from an annual growth rate of 11.7% at its worst in 1974, to only 5.0% at its best in late 1976—a slowdown of 6.7 percentage points. In the more recent period, the CPI slowed from 10.8% annual growth to 3.2%, a decline of 7.6 points.

In both cases, moreover, the slowdown in inflation occurred largely in three areas: food prices, energy prices, and mortgage interest rates. Changes in these areas have a lot to do with recessions and government policy, but not much to do with wage levels.

In the mid-1970s, food price increases were slowed by 10 percentage points, and energy prices by almost 28%, as seen in column 3 of the table. The huge change in energy prices, of course, reflects the end of the first oil crisis: in 1974, prices were still soaring, while by 1976 they had settled down. Mortgage rates actually stopped climbing and started to fall, slowing down by more than 18 percentage points, as monetary policy eased up.

	(1) 1974 III	(2) 1976 IV	(3) Change: (1)-(2)	(4) 1981 III	(5) 1983 II	(6) Change: (4)-(5)
Table 6: The Slowdown in Inflation, 1974-76 and 1981-83						
Consumer prices (all items)	11.7	5.0	6.7	10.8	3.2	7.6
Food	11.3	0.9	10.4	7.2	2.2	5.0
Energy	33.8	6.0	27.8	12.2	3.3	8.9
Mortgage interest	15.7	-2.9	18.6	27.5	-9.7	37.2
All other prices	7.5	6.7	0.8	9.1	5.7	3.4
Hourly compensation	9.7	8.0	1.7	9.4	5.6	3.8

Notes: Roman numerals in column headings refer to quarter-years; for instance, III means July to September. All figures in columns 1,2,4, and 5 are percent changes from one year earlier. Prices are the consumer price index (CPI-W) and its components, as published in the Bureau of Labor Statistics monthly press releases..The CPI-W was used because the treatment of housing and mortgage rates in the more common CPI-U was totally changed in January 1983. Hourly compensation includes wages, payroll taxes and some fringe benefits, as reported in the BLS *Monthly Labor Review.*

(The negative entry, -2.9%, in column 2 of the table means that in late 1976, mortgage rates were 2.9% lower than a year earlier.)

The next time around, in the 1980s, the changes in food an energy prices, while still important, were not quite as large. Food prices slowed by 5%, and energy prices by almost 9%, as seen in column 6 of the table. But the change in mortgage rates was immense. In 1981, at the height of Volcker's tight money policy, mortgage rates were rising more than 27% annually; by mid-1983, in the new era of easy money, mortgage rates were almost 10% lower than a year earlier. The net change, therefore, was 37 percentage points.

Most of the relief from inflation achieved in both recessions is due to the changes in these three volatile items. Unemployment and lower incomes have driven down the demand for food and energy, dampening further price increases; and the government itself, by easing up on monetary policy, is able to bring mortgage rates down during recessions. But there is little evidence here for the familiar conservative claim that wage increases are the cause of inflation. It is hard to see how changes in wage gains have led to the rapid fluctuations in food prices, energy prices, or mortgage rates.

Wage changes should have more influence on the prices of other items such as manufactured goods and services. But in contrast to the zig-zagging prices of food, energy and mortgages, the prices of all other items appear positively placid. All other components of the consumer price index barely slowed at all in the mid-1970s, dropping only from a 7.5% growth rate to 6.7%, for a slowdown of less than one percentage point. The Reagan recession had somewhat greater impact, slowing "all other prices" by 3.4 percentage points.

Similarly, Reagan did more to slow the growth of labor costs. Hourly compensation, a measure including wages, payroll taxes and some fringe benefits, slowed by 1.7 percentage points in the mid-1970s, but by 3.8 percentage points in the early 1980s. This is the statistical measure of the wrenching changes in labor relations described in this chapter. For employers, the wage slowdown was welcome news, evidence that Reagan had made good on his promise to whip inflation as they understood it.

For the rest of us, was it worth it? The secret of Reagan's success in fighting inflation was this: first, the Federal Reserve eased up on its previous policy of tight money, bringing interest rates down; second, the recession depressed demand for food and energy, holding down those volatile prices; and finally, all other prices, and labor costs, slowed down by between 3 and 4 percentage points—or 2 percentage points more than last time around. For this, we endured 10% unemployment, the devastation of cities and industries, the massacre of the federal budget.

Moreover, will it last? In the mid-1970s, slower inflation lasted only for the first 18 months of recovery. Today, nothing has changed to prevent food and energy prices from taking off again, when and if the recovery goes far enough. The Federal Reserve could easily decide that tight money was once again called for. Even the modest reduction in other prices and labor costs could be blown away by renewed economic growth.

The president who presided over the mid-1970s reduction in inflation was named Gerald Ford. No one today remembers him as the man who licked inflation once and for all. Ronald Reagan will be remembered differently than Gerald Ford, for many reasons: far from inability to walk and chew gum at the same time, our current leader seems capable of simultaneously eating jelly beans and invading the Caribbean, for example. But as inflation-fighters, both Reagan and Ford may be headed for similarly obscure fates. Their gains, so painfully won, are written on sand, destined to be washed away by the waves of a few years of recovery.

chapter 10

new
liberals
for
old

*Some people call me an Atari Democrat. Actually, I'm
a Wang Democrat.*
　　　　　　　　　—Senator Paul Tsongas, 1983

Paul Tsongas likes to offer his hometown of Lowell,
Massachusetts as a model for America's future. Lowell had been
an important center of the nineteenth-century textile industry,
but turned into just another declining mill town for much of the
twentieth century. Then in the 1970s, municipal officials set out
to revitalize the city and attract new businesses. Today Lowell is
the proud home of the headquarters and some of the production
facilities of Wang Laboratories, a fast-growing computer company.

Tsongas is, in contemporary jargon, a "neo-liberal." This
species also includes Senators Gary Hart of Colorado and Bill
Bradley of New Jersey, Representatives Richard Gephardt of
Missouri and Tim Wirth of Colorado, and a growing number of
other Democratic politicians. They are "neo" because of their
search for alternatives to Roosevelt- or Kennedy-style old
liberalism. Reliance on labor unions and traditional reform
movements, and emphasis on completion of the welfare state and
maintenance of full employment, are no longer enough for the
new breed of liberals. Their fascination with high-technology,
high-growth industries earned them the label of "Atari Democrats"—back when Atari was a rapidly growing company, that is.

143

For neo-liberals the top priorities are boosting economic growth and restoring U.S. competitiveness with Europe and Japan. To that end, they argue, the government should foster the development of "sunrise industries," the high-technology growth sectors of the future, through increased research funding, a new public development bank, and an array of more traditional incentives as well. In addition, Washington needs to build up the decaying infrastructure of highways, railroads, public utilities and the like, to make industrial growth possible. Better public education and job training should be oriented to the new employment opportunities. To ease workers out of declining, "sunset" industries, and to defuse opposition to the new pattern of growth, generous retraining, relocation and adjustment assistance are called for.

This sounds far more humane and sensible than Reaganomics. But neo-liberalism is not fundamentally a humanitarian or democratic viewpoint. Its goal is to equip the economy to fight more fiercely in world trade. Meeting human needs at home is a secondary concern, to be tolerated only to the extent permitted by the state of the trade wars. Spending priorities would often have to be set by marketing experts and technical researchers, not by popular vote. Less bizarre, less blatantly biased than Reaganomics, neo-liberalism still places the needs of business at the head of the nation's agenda; it still puts key decisions in the hands of an undemocratic elite.

Neo-liberalism will be a hot topic for election-year debates, both in 1984 and for some time to come. It is worth looking at the development of these ideas, in the writings of a number of economists. There are three places, in particular, to look: at the work of Ira Magaziner and Robert Reich; of Lester Thurow; and of Felix Rohatyn.

Outmanaging Japan

For an elaborate and well-argued presentation of neo-liberalism, there is no better place to start than *Minding America's Business*, by Ira Magaziner and Robert Reich[1]. Magaziner is a consultant to businesses in the U.S. and abroad; Reich was on the staff of the Federal Trade Commission during the Carter administration, and is now a Harvard professor. Although they clearly write from a liberal perspective, their sole focus is on helping American companies win the battles of foreign trade.

The first half of *Minding America's Business* is a grand tour of U.S. management failures. According to Magaziner and Reich, foreign (usually Japanese, sometimes European) companies plan farther ahead in almost every way. They are more willing to make big investments and set low initial prices in order to gain a foothold in foreign markets, even at the cost of low short-run profits. Their accounting systems reflect accurately the economies of scale that can be achieved in growing markets, while U.S. accounting often understates these advantages. Foreign companies of necessity pay more attention to their competitors around the world; U.S. managers for too long imagined that their only real rivals were at home. In some products, foreign firms have opted for more expensive design, production and inspection standards—a choice which pays off in a long-run reputation for high quality, and in lower costs for repairs under warranty.

Numerous persuasive-sounding anecdotes are offered to illustrate these points, although the skeptical reader has to take them on faith: almost all are based on anonymous "client studies" by Magaziner's consulting firm, with the identities of the companies, and sometimes even the products, concealed. Still, it is a plausible account of some of the ways in which American business has gone wrong. And it is an optimistic account, largely blaming correctible errors of judgment, rather than U.S. wage levels, environmental regulations, or taxes.

For example, in color television production, Magaziner and Reich found that, in 1979, a U.S. producer had slightly lower wages than the Japanese companies ($8.22 vs. $8.50 an hour). Moreover, the U.S. company had close to half the labor done overseas at $1.04 an hour; the Japanese had very little labor done outside their main plants. But despite higher hourly labor costs, the Japanese used superior product designs which required much less labor, and thus lower wage costs, per television set. In such cases, catching up to Japanese design and production technique, not slashing wages, seems the obvious solution.

The second half of *Minding America's Business* is about the need for an "industrial policy"—a public plan for restructuring the nation's industry. At present the patchwork of government policy does too much to protect inefficient industries through tariffs and other barriers to imports, but too little to ease labor and capital out of these industries and into growing areas. The allocation of research spending, government subsidies, loan guarantees and other aids to business reflects the patterns of political clout, not any explicit judgment about which industries are most promising. Pentagon procurement and research funding has built up such key industries as computers, semiconductors and aircraft, but only as a byproduct of military goals; this is far from a conscious industrial policy.

Other countries, particularly Sweden, West Germany and Japan, do much better on all these points. Foreign governments have even tried to anticipate which industries will soon start to decline. They have then discouraged further investment, and steered workers toward other jobs, before the industries' profits, production and employment come crashing down in a recession. And virtually all other industrial countries provide much better adjustment and retraining programs for the unemployed than the U.S. does.

So Magaziner and Reich conclude that in industrial policy, as in television design, the U.S. needs to catch up with its foreign competition. They advocate measures to ease labor adjustment to industrial change, including better retraining programs, requirement of advance notification of plant shutdowns, and special aid to depressed regions of the country. They want an increase in civilian research and development funding, with a more conscious focus on promising growth industries. Long-term planning is needed, too, for industries which are vital to the health of the rest of the economy—areas such as steel, machine tools and semiconductors. Magaziner and Reich favor the creation of a public development fund, able to make long-term, low-interest loans to important ventures. Finally, they call for a greatly expanded government role in promoting exports as an alternative, in most cases, to restrictions on imports.

All in all, the industrial policy proposed by Magaziner and Reich is, as they themselves suggest, a liberal answer to the supply-side question:

> . . . supply-siders are now asking how investment can increase our standard of living. The question is appropriate. It is their answer that is wrong.[2]

(In contrast to *Minding America's Business*, Reich's later book, *The Next American Frontier*[3], is a disappointment. Less rooted in industrial reality, it is more given to grand overstatement and wild optimism about the potential of new technology.

For understanding the neo-liberal argument, the earlier book is the more important one.)

Win some, lose some

Another neo-liberal view of the problems of growth is provided by MIT economist Lester Thurow. In *The Zero-Sum Society*[4], Thurow offers an eclectic, wide-ranging survey of the economic woes of the 1970s and a batch of policy proposals for the 1980s. The title refers to a metaphor which runs through the book: most economic and political conflicts are "zero-sum games," like poker, in which one person can win only what another loses. According to Thurow, this accounted for the political paralysis of the 1970s, since potential losers were so successful in blocking virtually all new policy proposals. Most solutions to the energy crisis or cures for inflation, he argues, would impose unacceptably large costs on some part of society. (Writing in 1979, he dismissed the "big bang" approach, stopping inflation via massive unemployment, as politically impossible; Congress and the voters, he thought, would not stand for it.)

Thurow, more than Magaziner and Reich, is concerned with economic theory as well as reality. Yet it is in the realm of theory that Thurow is curiously inconsistent. At times he argues passionately against the notion that unfettered private enterprise could solve all our problems; at other times he lines up with the mainstream of the economics profession, attacking ignorant reformers who fail to appreciate the beauty of the marketplace. The amalgamation of these opposite views, with no apparent logical connection, may be what inspired *Business Week* to call the book "ruthlessly honest" and "tough-minded"; in fact, the inconsistencies make the book unnecessarily tough reading.*

Problems of wages, employment and income distribution bring out the liberal side of Thurow. His critique of the idea that the free market and fluctuating wages could lead to full employment, summarized briefly in Chapter 9 above, is a model of clarity. Since work in a large enterprise is a complex,

---

*It is possible that Thurow's views are changing. His later book, *Dangerous Currents*[5], is more consistently critical of free-market theory. However, it is a book solely about economic theory, with nothing to say about policy. Thurow's reputation as a leading neo-liberal rests on *The Zero-Sum Society*.

interdependent process, with many important skills learned only on the job, workers must be motivated to cooperate with each other and to train new employees. This requires fairly rigid wages and seniority-based systems of hiring, firing and promotions—whether or not unions have demanded such policies. Because important skills must be learned at work, Thurow continues, equality of formal education does not create equality of opportunity. Government action to achieve full employment is necessary. Racial and sexual income inequality, problems to which Thurow repeatedly returns, can only be eliminated by direct government action.

However, Thurow is peeved at the environmental movement. All those silly regulations keep getting in the way of growth. (That's the sort of ruthless honesty that goes over big in the business world.) High prices, not regulations, are the way to achieve conservation of energy and other scarce resources. If some regulations are inevitable, we should at least understand the futility of trying to regulate production directly. Instead, the preferred marketplace solution is to influence business indirectly with taxes, subsidies, and effluent charges (fees for pollution—so much per pound of each kind of waste released into the air or water). Such regulations are superior because they are compatible with the logic of private enterprise, although Thurow does note that market solutions may be difficult to find for substances that cause cancer.

On the question of economic growth, Thurow sounds similar to Magaziner and Reich. Many of the same themes are stressed: the need for faster movement of labor and capital from declining ("sunset") to rising ("sunrise") industries, or for more and better-focused research. In terms of policy, Thurow favors the elimination of regulations, subsidies and government protection of industry. And he calls for active government involvement in investment planning, to ensure future energy supplies and to strengthen the sunrise industries.

However, he argues that extensive compensation of the losers from such policies will be necessary, to prevent them from creating political obstacles and bringing the economy to a halt once again. Since environmental regulation cannot be entirely defeated, businesses should stop wasting time trying, and should get on with building new plants more quickly, even with some added pollution control costs. More importantly, progressive taxation and government income supports and employment programs will be needed. Thurow favors a guarantee of public employment, with wages and promotion opportunities similar to those in private enterprise, for anyone who wants to work—and income support at about half the average wage for those who are unable to work.

Bigger MACs and smaller paychecks

If Lester Thurow, Ira Magaziner and Robert Reich sound like liberal intellectuals talking to business, Felix Rohatyn is unmistakably a banker talking to liberals. And not just any banker: he headed the bail-out operation which saved New York City from bankruptcy in its 1975 crisis. Rohatyn's message, expounded in numerous magazine articles (many of them in the *New York Review of Books*), is that the larger economic problems of the 1980s are quite similar to those faced by New York—and the solutions, too, should be similar.

The New York budget crisis resulted from a combination of unusually extensive municipally-financed social services, a declining tax base, a bit of creative accounting which papered over the early signs of trouble, and the 1975 recession, which lowered tax revenues while increasing the demand for services. The city came perilously close to defaulting on the interest payments on its bonds, and was unable to borrow any more money to meet its ongoing deficit. In response the state government created the Municipal Assistance Corporation ("Big MAC"), chaired by Rohatyn, to take over the city's finances. Backed by state and federal guarantees, Big MAC could still raise money for the city by selling bonds. Since the MAC board was dominated by corporate executives and state officials, it was insulated from the pressures of New York City politics, and free to demand unpopular budget cuts in return for money.

Rohatyn has no illusions about what Big MAC did to the city. In his words,

> When government cutbacks occur, the needy always get hurt. New York City was kept out of bankruptcy by a wage freeze, a 20 percent reduction in manpower, shifts in pension costs, a tuition charge at the City University, transit fare increases, and savage cost control, coupled with a variety of state tax cuts, and inflation driven

> revenue increases; but it was the lower-income families
> that got hurt. This result is unfair, but it is to some
> degree inevitable....[6]

Other neo-liberals may dream of industrial policies that lead to
rapid growth; for Rohatyn, New York's agony proved that
salvation is achieved through suffering:

> Sacrifice was demanded from all the different elements
> among our citizens and if, as is inevitable, sacrifice is
> always greater among our underprivileged, at least an
> attempt was made to be fair and most people gave up
> something.[7]

If Rohatyn calls this success, one shudders to imagine his idea of
failure.

National economic problems look much the same, only
larger, to Rohatyn; and of course a bigger apple requires a Bigger
MAC. He advocates a domestic economic summit, at which
everyone would agree to give up something. The administration
and Congress would have to accept tax increases and sharp
budget cuts; the Federal Reserve would agree to lower interest
rates; labor and management would allow limits on wage and
price increases; and the beginnings of an industrial policy would
be forged. The public, evidently, would have to give up the idea of
voting on how its tax dollars get spent—such decisions, as in New
York after the crunch, would be made by bankers and other
political and economic heavyweights.

Wholehearted endorsement of the economics of pain makes
it easy for Rohatyn to produce specific policy proposals. A 50c a
gallon increase in gasoline taxes would cut oil imports, and keep
the auto industry and its customers focused on the desirability of
small cars. Social Security and Medicare must be slashed, but so
must the defense budget. An absolutely universal draft, with very
low wages for draftees, would cut Pentagon costs through
democratically distributed sacrifice.

But Rohatyn's real love lies elsewhere, in his plan for a
public development bank. The model is the Reconstruction
Finance Corporation of the 1930s, which loaned money to
troubled businesses and public agencies. It saved many enterprises
from collapse, and even returned a small profit to the taxpayers.
Rohatyn's other proposals for tax hikes and budget cuts would
make money available to start a new R.F.C. Like the earlier

version, the new R.F.C. would loan public money to key industries, and to local government efforts to rebuild the country's crumbling infrastructure. Like New York's Big MAC, the R.F.C. would be intentionally insulated from democratic political control, so that it could demand unpopular concessions:

> In the industrial field, the R.F.C.'s investments would be limited to those basic industries such as automobiles and steel that could be made competitive. The R.F.C. would provide funds only if there were concessions on the part of labor, management, suppliers and bankers sufficient to make the company competitive with the best foreign producers.

> Similarly, in the public-infrastructure field the R.F.C.'s capital would be available only if local support—such as tax changes, union productivity and wage concessions, fare and user fees—assured the viability of the projects. These would include mass-transit systems, sewers, roads, bridges and so on.[8]

As this last quote suggests, Rohatyn emphasizes the need to rebuild the old basic industries such as auto and steel, and to prevent the collapse of the older urban centers of the Northeast and Midwest. The industries involved are too big to discard; as he points out, the auto industry is one of the largest markets for microprocessors, industrial robots and other high-tech paraphernalia. No heavy industry means less, not more, high-tech growth. The cities, too, cannot be abandoned: too much of the nation's population and industrial capacity, too many centers of transportation, finance and culture, are found in the old urban areas of the "Frost Belt." Unlike Ronald Reagan, Felix Rohatyn has a plan for saving the older parts of the country; however, that plan relies heavily on conscious, coordinated shrinkage of wages and services, with those on the bottom "inevitably" being squeezed the tightest.

Once you've got a good idea, you might as well use it as often as possible. Writing about the threat of international financial crisis if Third World countries default on their debts, Rohatyn suggests that the problem "is not unlike that faced by New York City in 1975." The solution is an international conference to coordinate plans for worldwide recovery, and a much-strengthened International Monetary Fund or similar agency, able to extract new concessions from debtor nations in return for loans and guarantees.[9] It would be the biggest MAC of all—at least until the development of interplanetary banking.

Meanwhile, back in Allentown

Would neo-liberalism work? Undoubtedly it would be superior to Reaganomics in many ways. Retraining, rather than repressing, the poor and the unemployed would be a vast improvement. The cheery versions of neo-liberalism suggest that everyone would soon be prospering. But even Rohatyn's grimly planned shrinkages might be preferable to Reagan's determination to steal lunch money from schoolchildren in order to feed the Pentagon. At one level, then, the response can only be, if neo-liberals have found the language in which sanity will start seeping back into Washington, more power to them.

At a deeper level, defects can be seen in neo-liberal economics. As a theory of what has gone wrong with the U.S. and what needs to be done to revive the economy, neo-liberalism has three interrelated flaws. First, it exaggerates the success of Japan. Second, it often overstates the potential of high-tech industry. And finally, it would orient our society toward nationalist rivalry with other countries, rather than toward meeting human needs and resolving existing conflicts within the U.S.

As the U.S. trade deficit has mounted in recent years, so, too, has the cult of "samurai management," the belief that Japanese business can do no wrong. Magaziner and Reich are not entirely free of this belief, although much worse versions can be found in the business section of any bookstore. In fact, Japan's fabled Ministry of International Trade and Industry (MITI) is not all-powerful. It tried for years to get Japan's nine auto makers merged into two or three big companies, without success. Nor is MITI always able to foresee the future: it persuaded Japanese chemical companies to invest in the production of new petro-chemicals in the 1960s; more recently it has urged the same companies to abandon those investments, since higher oil prices have made them unprofitable.

Or, to take a currently trendy example, there have been countless dire warnings that the Japanese are winning a larger share of the market for each successive generation of computer chips. For the coming generation (the "256K RAM chip"), it was thought that U.S. producers might be shut out entirely. Then suddenly, in mid-1983, it was discovered that Western Electric was far ahead of both Japanese and other American competition in 256K RAM chip development. A senior manager at Toshiba, a Japanese producer, called Western Electric "a very formidable competitor," and said, "We're kind of afraid of their potential." Shattering still more stereotypes, Western Electric produces all its chips at unionized plants in old Pennsylvania industrial cities. Its largest facility, which it is expanding, is in Allentown—a city thought to be so dead that it was featured in a 1982 popular song about factory closings.[10]

There are, of course, many areas in which the U.S. has lost out to Japanese competition, and many lessons to be learned—as Magaziner and Reich make clear—from foreign business. But even the huge U.S. trade deficit with Japan reflects more prosaic features as well, such as the high value of the dollar relative to the yen. This makes U.S. goods expensive in Japan, and Japanese goods cheap in the U.S. The high value of the dollar is in part a result of recession and high interest rates in the early 1980s; recovery and lower interest rates should bring down the value of the dollar, and bring down some of the Japanese trade advantage along with it.[11]

Like the threat from Japan, the potential of high technology is often painted larger than life-size. Countless communities are looking to new technologies for jobs and prosperity. Akron, Ohio, long famous as the center of the rubber industry, lost its last tire plant in 1982; it is now advertising itself as "Polymer Valley" in the hopes of attracting chemical companies.

A few will succeed, but most cities will be disappointed in such hopes for the future. New technologies are transforming industry, but they are not creating many jobs. Both government and private forecasters predict that, from 1983 to 1993, high-tech industries will create no more than a million new jobs—less than half the number lost in manufacturing from 1980 to 1982. Of those million jobs in high-tech industry (a broadly defined category, including drugs, chemicals, petroleum refining and aircraft, as well as computers, electronics and equipment), only a third will involve technical skills. Most will be in traditional clerical and blue-collar occupations. There will be some high-tech jobs in other industries—perhaps a quarter-million computer programmers over the next decade—but these, too, do not add up to an answer to unemployment or a strategy for growth.[12]

As Rohatyn recognizes, the growth of high-technology products rests on the strength of other industries. Computers, semiconductors and related technologies are becoming ever more widely used in office and factory automation, and in Pentagon preparations for futuristic forms of destruction. (Serious moves toward disarmament, in fact, might hurt some high-tech fields, unless government spending on related civilian technologies were stepped up.)

Beside such major uses, sales of high-tech consumer products seem insignificant—and undependable. Throughout 1981 and most of 1982, Atari's sales of video games and home computers soared while most of the economy sagged. Atari was opening new factories and hiring workers at a time of 10% unemployment; it was in this era that the neo-liberal wing of the Democratic Party was informally named after the company. Then in late 1982, sales and profits abruptly plummeted. In 1983 Atari closed a factory built only a year earlier, laid off at least 1700 employees, and moved its assembly operations to Hong Kong and Taiwan. Union organizers began showing up at the gates of the remaining Atari plants; the label of "Atari Democrats" vanished almost overnight. A successful cigarette marketing executive was brought in to head Atari, in the hope that his prowess in hooking consumers on addictive products could be transferred to the video screen.[13] Aside from such passing consumer fads, high technology will remain largely something used by other industries, and dependent on them for growth.

Not all variants of neo-liberalism share the fascination with high-tech alternatives or Japanese management. Rohatyn provides a sober rejoinder to his colleagues on these points. But all do agree that what we, as a nation, should be about is beating other nations in trade. This notion is problematical in several respects. It can easily reinforce the ugly aspects of nationalist rivalry: the public demolitions of Japanese cars, the occasional incidents of hostility and violence toward Orientals in Midwestern cities, are an ominous warning of where this road could lead us.

Moreover, the priority given to international trade is the reason why neo-liberalism is ultimately undemocratic. Government spending and other public policy questions become technical problems, to be decided by trade experts. As Thurow says, "If you really think that Americans are so incompetent that they cannot pick sunrise industries, then you can simply use the Japanese list."[14]

There is no room here for the possibility that the U.S. might have different priorities than Japanese business. Nor is there any hint of attempting to reduce our dependence on trade, of steering capital and labor into construction of housing and public facilities, expansion of social services, and other necessarily local forms of production. (For more on this, see Chapter 12.)

Believing that we are all in this together, in the great national crusade to stomp on our foreign competitors, neo-liberalism also overlooks the existence of basic conflicts within the U.S. Magaziner and Reich offer the most upbeat variant, in which Japanese management techniques and Swedish welfare programs will unite us all in growth. Thurow, despite the title of his book and his long reflections on "zero-sum" political conflicts, ends up proposing to businessmen that they can best restore profitable growth by cutting a deal with their critics. Share a little of the prosperity with women and minorities, spend a little more on pollution control, he urges, and the wheels will turn more smoothly—to everyone's benefit. (Or, as Paul Tsongas puts it, "The business community used to look at Democrats, with some validity, as well-meaning imbeciles. What we're trying to do now is tell business, 'We can be trusted with the economy.' "[15]) Even Rohatyn is riding the same elevator, although he claims it always goes down a few floors before it starts upward.

Trade wars, like the genuine blood-and-bullets variety, evidently must take precedence over purely internal conflicts. The clash of management vs. labor in the workplace, protests over racism and sexism, the defense of environmental regulations, the battle between upper-income taxpayers and lower-income service recipients—all this is to be put aside until we get ahead of Japan. If all goes well, the optimism of Magaziner, Reich and Thurow may be justified, and everyone may get their share. If, like the supply-side miracle of Reaganomics, the neo-liberal solution takes a little longer than advertised, we can always call on Rohatyn.

Neo-liberalism is less cruel, less prejudiced against the poor, less committed to strangely mistaken logic than is Reaganomics. Yet it is still far from an adequate answer to our economic ills. Lowell, Massachusetts, the model of high-tech success proposed by Paul Tsongas, is lucky rather than typical. Lowell is within 30 miles of Harvard and MIT; it has many vacant factories; and it received a new wave of foreign immigrants in the 1970s, who were willing to work for minimum wages. Even so, the Lowell success story has scarcely extended beyond the downtown business section; the aging, deteriorating residential areas have yet to share in the city's rebirth. This is not a pattern of growth which can rebuild the shattered expanses of the American economy.

chapter 11

economic democracy

[Capitalism] is not a success. It is not intelligent, it is not beautiful, it is not just, it is not virtuous—and it doesn't deliver the goods. In short, we dislike it, and we are beginning to despise it. But when we wonder what to put in its place, we are extremely perplexed...
—John Maynard Keynes, 1933[1]

Is capitalism itself the cause of our economic problems? Today, as in the depths of the Great Depression, the idea is becoming increasingly plausible. No mere tinkering will restore lasting prosperity. None of the major policy alternatives seem adequate to the 1980s: the varieties of conservative policy have failed quite dramatically; old-fashioned liberalism has faded away, and its neo-liberal replacement looks problematical. But, like Keynes in the 1930s, many modern critics of capitalism lack a clear vision of an alternative.

In another country or another era, the alternative would naturally have been described as socialism. Unlike most industrial capitalist countries, however, we do not have a sizeable socialist movement. And the most familiar example of socialism, the Soviet Union, provides an obviously unattractive model (even when freed of the usual mass-media caricatures). So the search for economic alternatives has been expressed in more traditional American terms—in terms of democracy.

Modern capitalism, in its good and bad years alike, is fundamentally undemocratic. Crucial decisions which shape the lives of millions of people are made by the impersonal forces of the market, or by remote, unresponsive managers at the pinnacles of corporate and government bureaucracies. Democratic political institutions often appear powerless to redirect the economy in line with the will of the majority.

A number of economists have suggested, therefore, that what we need is "economic democracy." Their proposals include democratic control of the workplace and guarantees of employment; public control of some investment decisions; and expanded, restructured government services and employment programs. Such measures, it is said, will democratize our economic institutions and, at the same time, will lift us out of the economic crisis of the past decade.

Even more than neo-liberalism, economic democracy is still primarily a set of ideas and proposals, found in books and articles rather than in legislation and political platforms. Three recent books, in particular, have helped to develop the idea of economic democracy: *The Deindustrialization of America*, by Barry Bluestone and Bennett Harrison[2]; *A New Social Contract*, by Martin Carnoy, Derek Shearer and Russell Rumberger[3]; and *Beyond the Waste Land*, by Samuel Bowles, David Gordon, and Thomas Weisskopf[4].

All three are insightful works which diagnose much of the present economic malaise quite persuasively. They are important steps toward understanding what needs to be done to the economy. Yet they are incomplete in a number of ways. Most importantly, they tend to minimize the difficulty of achieving economic democracy, and understate the extent of the changes their proposals would require. This chapter presents a review and friendly critique of these leading works on economic democracy. The next chapter suggests what it would take to complete the task these authors have started.

Capital vs. community

In *The Deindustrialization of America*, Bluestone and Harrison tackle the same question as the neoliberals: what industrial policies will revitalize the American economy? But while neoliberals like Thurow and Reich call for faster movement of capital into newly promising fields, Bluestone and Harrison argue just the opposite. The rapid flight of investment and jobs from one city, industry or country to another imposes great human costs. Far from being the solution, capital mobility is a large part of the problem for workers and communities. There is a maximum "socially manageable velocity" of capital, and business should be prevented from exceeding that speed limit.

Capital has indeed been moving rapidly, as Bluestone and Harrison document with remarkable thoroughness. From 1969 to 1976—before the recent wave of auto, steel and other plant closings—openings of new business establishments created 25 million jobs in the U.S., while closings destroyed 22 million jobs. Even among manufacturing plants with 100 or more employees in 1969, fully 30% had been shut down by 1976; interestingly, this percentage was slightly higher in the South (34%) than elsewhere. The fact that a region like the South is generally growing does not mean that any particular job or community within it is economically secure.

Job loss has severe effects on workers and their communities. Study after study has found that many victims of plant closings remain jobless long after their unemployment benefits run out. Those who do find work usually suffer sharp declines in income and occupational status. Physical and mental health suffer as well: sustained unemployment leads to predictable increases in heart attacks, cirrhosis of the liver, suicides, homicides, mental hospital and prison admissions. The "ripple effects" of plant closings include contraction or bankruptcies of neighboring small businesses, as they lose their paying customers, and cutbacks in public services, as the local tax base declines.

Rapid capital mobility is bad for the rising communities as well as the falling, for Houston as well as Detroit. Explosive, unplanned urban growth has led to staggering traffic jams in Houston, and to belated interest in developing mass transit. Meanwhile, as recently as 1978, one-fourth of the city's streets were unlighted, and 400 miles of streets were unpaved. Other Sunbelt boomtowns suffer other problems of too-rapid growth: the collapse of the water table in Florida or the growth of air pollution in the Southwest threaten to undermine the fabled quality of life that helped draw people there in the first place.

When new industries do arrive, they do not usually employ those who were left behind by earlier slumps. New England, until the 1970s famous for its ever-declining textile, clothing and shoe mills, was suddenly "saved" by the boom in high-technology industry. Yet a massive study of New England workers found that of those working in the mills in 1958 who later lost their jobs, fewer than 3% were employed in high-tech industries in 1975. The new industries require new skills, and typically hire younger, highly educated people rather than retraining old millworkers.

Bluestone and Harrison argue that the extraordinary rate of capital mobility has been based on "permissive" technologies developed since World War II: faster freight transportation, culminating in the wide-bodied cargo jet; and faster communication, ultimately the worldwide linkage of a company's computers via satellite. These techniques allow materials and information to be moved around the globe at will, permitting nationwide and worldwide coordination of corporate activities as never before. Ultimately, the new techniques permit the movement of many jobs to the lowest-wage corners of the Third World.

Even in the 1950s and 1960s, when an informal (if grudging) truce between capital and labor was in effect, big business was expanding fastest in the non-union Sunbelt and abroad. Though employment grew, in absolute terms, almost everywhere, the share of production done in the older, unionized areas of the U.S. was dropping.

In the 1970s, as foreign competition intensified and profits declined, corporations accelerated their movement of capital and called off the truce with labor. With increasing capital mobility came increasing demands for wage concessions from workers, and for tax concessions from states and localities. Yet differences in local tax rates were almost never decisive for business profitability. In 1975 the effective rate of state and local taxation of business profits was 1.31% in both Texas and Ohio; the highest rate in a major industrial state was only 2.75%, in Massachusetts.

Taxes, then, could not explain why corporations were more willing to expand in Texas than Ohio. But wages were another story. As a business consultant specializing in plant location told the *Wall Street Journal*, "Labor costs are the big thing, far and away. Nine times out of ten you can hang it on labor costs and unionization." The business solution to the economic crisis was to leave, to deindustrialize those areas where workers had won improvements in wages, work rules, and standards of living.

In response, Bluestone and Harrison propose strong plant-closing legislation, requiring advance notification, negotiation, and compensation of the affected workers and municipalities.

Beyond such defensive measures, they call for economic planning to create a radical industrial policy. When government aid is required, either to launch a "sunrise" industry or to save a "sunset" one, the public should gain a share of ownership in the industry in return for its tax dollars. Long-term planning agreements should be negotiated with private producers of essential products, and a variety of new public enterprises—local health clinics, for instance—should be created to supply public goods and services.

When companies close still-viable plants, the government should support worker and community efforts to buy and operate the enterprises. When a plant is no longer viable in its old industry, attempts should be made to "recycle" it, to find new products that the same workers can make in the same facilities. There will be many problems in implementing these proposals, but they are superior to the present approach of throwing away so much of our human and material resources year after year.

Bluestone and Harrison have done an exceptional job of analyzing one crucial part of the economic crisis. Yet they may have somewhat overstated their case. The pursuit of lower wages is an important motivation for capital mobility, but not the only one. A study of the recent patterns of U.S. foreign investment, by Arthur MacEwan,[5] found that companies move overseas most often to be close to their markets. Thus the fastest-growing area of foreign investment, ever since World War II, has been in Europe, where wages have risen rapidly and are now (in several countries) comparable to U.S. levels. Even when capital moves to the Third World, it may be in search of markets rather than cheap labor: in the late 1970s, 90% of the products made by U.S. companies in Mexico were sold in Mexico.

The difference is of more than academic interest. If the problem is that capital moves in pursuit of cheaper labor, perhaps we are forced to "save our jobs from them." There is an uncomfortable undercurrent of nationalism at times in Bluestone and Harrison's discussion of international capital flight.

If, on the other hand, capital often moves in order to be nearer to markets, then there is less reason to think that one nation's workers are pitted against another. Many jobs simply must be located where the products will be sold, whether it is the U.S., Europe, or Mexico. The need to produce near the market reflects both the strength of nationalist regulation of foreign business, and the limits to worldwide integration. Bluestone and Harrison's vision of wide-bodied cargo jets and worldwide computer networks may still be well beyond the reach of most businesses.

Even for those who could afford international integration, successful marketing may well require that a corporation be immersed in the national language and culture where its products are sold. So companies that do much selling abroad may eventually move some of their operations abroad as well. (Correspondingly, a number of Japanese companies that sell a lot in the U.S. have started to produce here.)

This critique, though, could itself be taken too far. There is no denying the importance of capital mobility, nor the severity of its human impact. And there is no better description of the issue available than the work of Bluestone and Harrison.

Hiring ourselves: the public payroll

While Bluestone and Harrison analyze the instability of private employment, Carnoy, Shearer and Rumberger stress the corresponding need for a much-expanded public sector. Private business decisions, made in pursuit of profits, have intensified the economic crisis of the 1970s and 1980s. To establish democratic control over the future course of the economy, Carnoy et al. suggest we should begin by recognizing that it is easier to control the actions of government than of business.

This leads Carnoy et al. to call for greater public investment. More public spending is needed to improve transportation, housing, health care, education and other basic services. On the other hand, a transfer of funds away from the military is desirable to increase the changes for peace, and to increase the funds available for other government activities.

Government spending has a dual function: it both improves public services and creates public employment. Carnoy et al. offer an interesting look at the pattern of government job creation. At present, one worker in six is employed by the public sector; over the past twenty years, one out of every four new jobs has been on the public payroll. Our taxes have gone, in no small measure, to hiring ourselves.

Important as it is for the whole society, public employment looms even larger for some groups. Black women and men (but not Hispanics) and white women are particularly likely to work for the government; more than a quarter of all black working women are in the public sector. Many highly educated workers— including about a third of all college graduates, and half of all black college graduates—are government employees.

Race and sex discrimination, while by no means absent, are less severe within the public sector. For example, among professionals, black females earn half as much as white males in the private sector, three-fourths as much in government. Other comparisons, for both professional and non-professional employees, show similar patterns. It seems that affirmative action policies are easier for the government to enforce in its own hiring than in the private sector.

The government also creates jobs indirectly when it buys things from private companies, as Carnoy et al. point out. The industries most dependent on government purchases include ordnance (weapons), aircraft, construction, chemicals, communications, and some business services. These industries tend to hire more white males (particularly skilled workers) and to have greater racial and sexual income inequality among their employees than the government itself. So government contracts have a very different meaning for employment than the government payroll. Based on this comparison, Carnoy et al. conclude that shifting funds from defense contracts to civilian government activities would create a more equal distribution of jobs and incomes—a major argument, they suggest, for disarmament.

Public investment and jobs are the beginning, but by no means the end, of economic democracy. In order to democratize investment funding, the federal government should buy a controlling interest in several banks and insurance companies; unions should seek to gain control over the uses of their pension funds; and the Federal Reserve should be made more open and accountable to the public. A democratic industrial policy would include support for employee ownership of firms, worker participation in management, and formation of new cooperative enterprises.

Other aspects of economic democracy would include environmental and worker protection, progressive tax reform, renewable energy development and the formation of a public energy corporation, improvements in social welfare programs, and international policies that support full employment and growth in the Third World. It is an inspiring list, and an extensive one.

There are, however, two major difficulties with economic democracy as portrayed by Carnoy, Shearer and Rumberger. The first arises in their analysis of public employment. It is useful to understand who is employed in government, as opposed to private industry, today. But it makes no sense to assume that such patterns must remain constant in the future, or to judge rival government programs by those patterns.

In particular, neither fans nor critics of the Reagan military budget really base their positions on the employment effects of Pentagon spending. If you believe military spending is crucial to protecting Our Way of Life, you will not be moved by hearing that it has unfortunately unequal effects on the labor market. On the other hand, if you believe that the arms race is a threat to the survival of human life, you will not endorse it just because it employs several million people. Analyses of the employment effects of the Pentagon budget have an uncanny tendency to agree with the authors' prejudices about militarism.

Carnoy et al., being opponents of military spending, suggest that it creates fewer jobs than other forms of spending, and disproportionately employs skilled white males. But other activities which they favor—school construction, or the development of high-speed trains, for instance—would have very similar employment patterns. It is not the militarism of the Pentagon that shapes its employment effects, so much as its reliance on construction, research and development, and production of experimental and small-batch items (requiring skilled machinists rather than assembly-line workers). Virtually all industrial policy proposals call for expanding such skilled activities, in one form or another.

Should the development of high-speed trains be discouraged, because so many of the jobs it would create would currently be done by skilled white males? Of course not. Even skilled white males have faced high unemployment in the 1980s; there is nothing wrong with the creation of job opportunities for them, so long as it does not prevent the creation of jobs for others as well. If an industrial policy is going to increase the need for construction, research and skilled machine work, surely it should be possible to open up access to these jobs. Getting more women and minorities into the building trades, or into scientific and technical training, would be no harder than many of the proposals made by Carnoy et al.

This raises the second major problem with economic democracy as it is presented in *A New Social Contract*. The proposals are a curious mixture of simple legislative reforms which might be achieved within the next few years, and long-term structural changes which are only imaginable after lengthy political battles. Too little is said about how these larger changes are to be achieved.

The authors seem to believe that what they present is largely a short-term program. Their description of the movements which might agitate for economic democracy is immersed in the immediate details of national politics in 1982-83. In introducing their program, Carnoy et al. write that

> The set of reform policies that we propose here are necessarily short-term, although they indicate a long-term direction for the economy. They speak most immediately to the next five to ten years.

But what is that indicated long-term direction for the economy? The authors seem almost proud of their vagueness; as they continue,

> [Our proposals] are not revolutionary; they will not lead to a perfect society. But they can bring about a substantially more decent and democratic form of a mixed economy. Whether this is labeled a more humane capitalism or a step toward democratic socialism, we leave to theorists.[6]

The question left to theorists here is not just a matter of labels. Implicitly at least, the question is whether economic democracy can exist while production and distribution are still dominated by traditional, privately owned big businesses. Is economic democracy a tailor with a new suit of clothes for corporate capitalism or the first visit from its gravedigger?

Carnoy et al. seem to lean toward the new suit of clothes option. They frequently describe corporate power as an obstacle to their plans; but equally often, they suggest that corporations could live with these proposals. An earlier book by two of the authors (*Economic Democracy*, by Carnoy and Shearer[7]) argued more explicitly for some sort of transformed capitalism:

> Under economic democracy, the rules of the market game would be changed: there would be more players

(cooperatives, worker-owned firms, community development corporations, public enterprises), and the relationships between the players would be more balanced. This kind of market actually resembles Adam Smith's laissez-faire vision of the "invisible hand" more than does the existing corporate-dominated U.S. economy.[8]

However, it is hard to envision the nation's largest corporations putting up with the proposals made by Carnoy et al. Democracy is an all-American idea, which everyone supports; but government takeover of a few big banks and insurance companies, and creation of a public energy-producing company, will separate the "economic democrats" from the capitalists among us. The package presented by Carnoy et al., as a whole, would be seen by capitalists as a frontal assault on their economic system. It would likely provoke a refusal to keep investing or even producing—in other words, a strike by capitalists.

What is needed, then, is not only an attractive set of proposals for economic democracy, but also a realistic plan for how to achieve it in the face of the likely opposition. The political strategy for such a transformation would involve building a long-term movement for change, far beyond the current reforms. The economic analysis would require a more systematic approach to dismantling and replacing private control of production. That kind of discussion would sound less like it was on the agenda for the next five years, but more like it could succeed someday.

Carnoy, Shearer and Rumberger have produced a useful analysis of government employment, and an interesting list of proposals for economic democracy. Yet while impressive in many specifics, it remains frustratingly vague about the theoretical picture behind it. In the end, the question of just what economic democracy is supposed to be, and how to get there, remains dangling.

Waste not, want not

For Samuel Bowles, David Gordon and Thomas Weisskopf, economic democracy is closer to being an alternative to capitalism. In *Beyond the Waste Land* they identify two closely linked, central problems: the continual waste of a huge fraction of our productive resources; and the slowdown in the growth of productivity (output per hour) since the late 1960s. Both problems are caused by corporate control of the economy, and by corporate strategies to maintain profits in difficult times. The answer to both problems is economic democracy. It would allow conversion from waste to useful production, and would create a more cooperative social environment in which productivity and incomes would rise.

Waste, in the eyes of Bowles et al., includes resources left idle, used ineffectively, or devoted to the production of useless goods and services. Some obvious examples are excess military spending, needlessly expensive health care, and the growth in advertising and packaging. Unemployment is clearly a waste: idle workers, factories and equipment could have been producing, instead of collecting benefits and gathering dust. Another form of waste is excess supervisory labor. The U.S. has far more supervisors per worker today than it did in the past—and far more than other industrial countries as well. In 1980, administrators and managers made up 10.8% of nonfarm labor here, compared to 3.0% in Germany and 4.4% in Japan.

An even deeper and perhaps larger source of waste is the lower motivation of workers in hierarchically-controlled enterprises. Studies of worker-controlled establishments have found that output per hour is 15% to 30% higher than in conventional firms. So Bowles et al. estimate that we lose at least 15% of our potential output due to "undemocratic production systems."

These numerous forms of waste add up to over a trillion dollars in 1980, or close to half of gross national product. The conclusion is that our economic problems stem not from a lack of resources, but from misdirected uses of what we have.

For Bowles et al., the decline in the rate of growth of productivity is at the heart of the economic crisis. Until the mid-1960s, output per worker seemed to be growing dependably at nearly 3% per year; since then, the growth has all but stopped. In *Beyond the Waste Land*, this slump is attributed to social conflicts over the role of corporate power. Three areas in particular—changes in innovative pressures on business, in popular resistance to corporate domination, and in the intensity of work—are said to explain the productivity slowdown.

The analysis of productivity offered by Bowles et al. is an uneven one; it is far more impressive in its broad sweep than in its statistical detail. On a qualitative, verbal level, they argue persuasively that social conflicts have important effects on productivity. But on the quantitative level, they present a hodge-podge of unconvincing evidence.

To measure innovative pressure on business, Bowles et al. use the rate of business failures. The idea, suggested by Joseph Schumpeter long ago, is that when new processes of production are being introduced, the business world is in turmoil, and the less successful and less innovative companies are likely to be driven into bankruptcy. The average efficiency of the economy then improves simply because the least efficient producers have been wiped out.

The notion that business failures are associated with innovation and productivity growth fits surprisingly well with the statistics before 1980. Business failures reached a peak in the early 1960s, a period of overall growth. The association of more failures with more growth seems less plausible, however, in the early 1980s, when extraordinary rates of bankruptcy accompanied little growth of productivity.

For the second social determinant of productivity, Bowles et al. end up proposing, strangely enough, that the costs of popular resistance to corporate power are partially reflected in the price of raw materials. Their measure of popular resistance, an index of raw materials prices, follows a familiar pattern: it drifts downwards throughout the 1950s and 1960s, jumps up quite abruptly in 1973, and jumps again in 1979 (see the graph on their page 138). This matches the movements in the price of crude oil quite closely; presumably their raw materials price index is dominated by the price of oil. Thus when they refer to the "cost of popular resistance" in their statistical analysis, they are largely measuring it with the price of oil—an ironic twist, since Bowles et al. argue strongly against theories which blame the economic crisis on oil prices.

The third social determinant of productivity is work intensity. The harder people work, the higher the output per hour. Bowles et al. argue quite effectively that the intensity of work is socially determined, dependent on such factors as the degree of supervision, fear of losing one's job, and anything else affecting worker motivation.

But their statistical measure of this concept sounds esoteric, and is never precisely defined: in the authors' own words,

> We multiplied the rate of supervision and the cost of losing your job to get a single variable reflecting

employer leverage over workers; we then combined this with . . .[an] index of inequality. . . and the percentage of workers represented by labor unions. In order to provide at least one proxy for worker motivation, we included the index of work safety. . .[9]

With this level of number-juggling, anything can be concocted. Neither the text nor the technical appendix ever describes exactly how or why Bowles et al. created this particular statistical measure of work intensity.

In short, all the detailed statistical work on the productivity slowdown looks shaky. Hopefully the important general point— that the productivity slowdown is related to socially determined changes in work intensity and in popular resistance to corporate power—will live on beyond the problematical statistical form in which it is presented here.

Beyond the Waste Land is more than an analysis of the U.S. economy. It also presents a program, a 24-point "economic bill of rights." The changes it calls for are sweeping ones: in terms of jobs, for instance, it proposes full employment at a sharply raised minimum wage, equal employment opportunity and narrowed wage differentials, public childcare, shorter work weeks and flexible hours, and a series of reforms aimed at democratizing workplaces.

Other proposals suggest numerous reforms, including democratic investment planning, direct Congressional control of the Federal Reserve, stiff environmental controls, reduced military spending, conservation and safe energy, national health care, and so on. One of the most innovative sections calls for community-based correctional programs, both because they would be more humane and because they would reduce crime control spending.

There are scattered problems and omissions in the proposals. In discussing price controls and tax reform, Bowles et al. sometimes seem trapped within the jargon and abstract schemes of the economics profession. Their treatment of international economic problems is vague. Their education proposal is solely concerned with expanding colleges and universities, overlooking the needs of elementary and secondary schools. But these are relatively minor flaws in a generally impressive document. More than any of the other works on the subject, *Beyond the Waste Land* makes economic democracy sound like a well-elaborated, and obviously attractive, system.

Yet the final question cannot be avoided. What kind of system is economic democracy? Is it compatible with corporate capitalism, or is it a replacement for private business? Bowles et al. stress the need for a grassroots political movement to agitate for and win the adoption of their program. At times, in the description of popular movements arrayed against "pro-business forces," they appear to be planning on total transformation of the economy.

At other times, however, they back off from this stance. Economic democracy, they say, will be as easy and accessible as participating in your local school board. Repeatedly, they announce that their program is affordable; if adopted it could pay for itself in two years. The appendix which explains this claim demonstrates that if full employment, rapid productivity growth, and a 50% reduction in military spending could be achieved in two years, we could all be better off and the government would have a lot of money to spend. This is arithmetically true, but politically dubious: little is said about the disruption which will accompany this two-year blitzkrieg if the "pro-business forces" refuse to cooperate. (A few concluding paragraphs do mention the possibility of business resistance, but only to suggest vaguely that this would make grassroots mobilization for economic democracy all the more important.) If taken literally, the Bowles et al. two-year plan is dangerously close to being the Laffer Curve of the left.

Reading the 24-point economic bill of rights offered in *Beyond the Waste Land*, it is hard to imagine it slipping into place in a smooth two-year transition. Despite the authors' occasional claims to the contrary, economic democracy is the beginning of a new economic system. It may appear politically expedient for the moment to deny this fact; but if the process of transformation gets underway, it will be essential to achieve greater clarity about just where we are going and how we plan to get there.

****

Economic democracy offers another, encouragingly different answer to the traditional debate between conservatives and liberals. The works that have appeared to date stress important themes including the costs of capital mobility, the size and role of public employment, the magnitude of waste and the social causes of slow productivity growth. The programs advocate a wide variety of changes that would democratize our economic institutions and create a chance for popular control of our economic future. Such changes would amount to a fundamental transformation—in general, more fundamental than the authors acknowledge.

The need for that deeper transformation of the economy is discussed in the next, and final, chapter.

chapter 12

people before profits

I think a lot of people look at us....as being overly aggressive. I would say that either you believe in the free enterprise system of this country, or you don't believe in it.
—Mobil Corporation Chairman Rawleigh Warner Jr.[1]

Mobil is not the only corporation which looks overly aggressive today. One company after another is enjoying newly won tax breaks, regulatory rollbacks, and employee concessions on wages and work rules. These corporate conquests have rested in large part on the actions of the Reagan administration. In effect, Reaganomics has insisted that the crisis of the U.S. economy can only be ended on terms dictated by big business. Different policies, ones which put people before profits, will require a very different solution to the long-term economic crisis.

As explained in Chapter 1, the crisis appeared in the 1970s because the bases of the post-World War II expansion eroded. U.S. international power was set back, militarily in Vietnam and economically in trade with Japan and Europe. The era of cheap oil came to an abrupt end, creating hardships for consumers and for many oil-hungry industries. The boom in automobiles and suburbanization slowed down. Changes in the nature of government intervention in the economy undercut former sources of corporate profits. The informal truce between management and labor was broken by a new era of workplace strife. The result of these changes was that growth in GNP per worker all but ceased, unemployment began to rise, and inflation spiralled upward.

Reaganomics has sought to restore growth and price stability through militarization of society and impoverishment of the working population. A no-nonsense projection of U.S. power abroad; getting the government out of social services and further into buying high-profit, high-technology hardware; driving down wages, working conditions and taxes; ending "environmental extremism"—all this, the story goes, should make it attractive for corporations to start investing and growing again. Eventually the prosperity will drip down onto the rest of us, but only if we first let those at the top splash about in it alone for quite a while.

Neo-liberalism proposes a different, less disastrous strategy, but one which still seeks above all else to rebuild business profits. Instead of a shooting war with the Soviet Union, the neo-liberals summon us to a trade war with Japan, to the task of outcompeting foreign industry. Never yet tested in practice, the more upbeat versions of neo-liberalism are likely far too optimistic about the potential of high-technology industry, the ease with which the U.S. can regain its former industrial lead, and the willingness of business to compromise with its critics. So neo-liberalism could quickly boil down to the kind of austere, planned shrinkages which Felix Rohatyn imposed on New York.

In short, acceptance of any of the mainstream economic philosphies will prove hazardous to our wealth. Neither the tax cut charlatans of the supply side, nor the free market mystics of monetarism, nor the trade war technicians of neo-liberalism will bring about full employment and income security for all Americans. For that we must look elsewhere, in less conventional directions.

Economic democracy, as seen in the last chapter, provides a start at a more promising strategy. Yet it appears too cowed by the "loyalty oath", the question posed by Mobil's Rawleigh Warner Jr. and so many others: do you believe in private enterprise, or don't you? Everyone knows the unspoken rule: if you don't believe, you are excommunicated from the mainstream, banished to wander on the fringes of political irrelevance.

To solve the economic crisis of the late twentieth century, we must overcome the fear of flunking capitalism's loyalty oath. Instead, the starting point should be a very different question. Do we have the ability to create a better way of life, to meet human needs more fully than our economy does at present? The answer is unmistakeably "yes." Then the next question is, what will it take to reorient the economy toward producing for people, toward satisfying the needs and desires of the majority of Americans? Once that has been answered, we can return to the private enterprise question in a new light. Is the alternative we seek compatible with capitalism, or not? Is private enterprise able to be loyal to *us*?

This chapter sketches the development of an alternative, an outline of an economic program that would put people before profits. In its early stages, it is quite similar to the proposals for economic democracy described above; in its later stages it aims to make clearer where such proposals are leading.

1: Finding the Funds

It has become fashionable in Washington to suggest that we, as a nation, are broke, that our highest economic priority must be reducing the deficit and spending less on everything. New initiatives seem out of the question, if we can scarcely afford the government programs we already have.

Any humane economic policy will cost a lot of money. Thus it must be understood at the outset that we are not broke. Deficits are a result, not a cause, of our economic problems. We can afford to feed the hungry, to cure the sick, to provide jobs rebuilding our cities and industries. But to do so we will have to reorganize our public finances; we must put the federal budget as rewritten by David Stockman far behind us.

Where will we find the funds for new programs? The answer will be hard to implement, but it is easy to describe. It has at least four parts.

First, military spending can be slashed. While our cities and social services are broke, the Pentagon is spending a million dollars every two minutes, day in and day out. Spending less on the military is important for more than just economic reasons; as the nuclear freeze movement points out, the very fate of the earth may depend on our success in achieving disarmament.

The Pentagon is, in fact, the fountain of waste which our government budget-cutters have been searching for. As seen in Chapter 5, it continually gushes forth weapons which none of us need, which serve no plausible defensive use. The human and material resources now wasted on warming up for war could go far toward peaceful economic reconstruction.

Second, a fair tax system should be created. For those in the upper brackets, the Reagan tax cuts were generous to a fault, as described in Chapter 3. But what is needed is not a return to the slightly less unfair tax schedules of the Carter era. Rather, we should start over almost from scratch, and draft a new tax code which is short and simple, which closes the countless existing loopholes, and which distributes the tax burden in proportion to ability to pay.

In the personal income tax, the exemption for each individual should be raised, almost all other exemptions and deductions should be eliminated, and two or three tax rates for incomes at different levels should be established. In the corporate income tax, Reagan's grab-bag of goodies for big business should be thrown out. In place of today's absurdly accelerated depreciation schedules and investment tax credits, there should be an honest accounting of corporate profits, and, as with individual taxes, a levy based on ability to pay.

Such a system would be far more fair, and far more widely understandable, than the present labyrinth of tax privileges, deductions, and accounting tricks. As a side benefit, it might free thousands of tax lawyers and accountants to engage in socially useful occupations. Most important, a reformed tax system would make it possible to raise more government revenue, without increasing the burden on those who can least afford to pay.

Third, a full employment policy (about which more below) would automatically generate increased revenues. Unemployment is expensive, not only to the unemployed but also to the government. When workers are laid off, they and their employers pay less in taxes; at the same time, many of the jobless receive government unemployment benefits, food stamps and other services. Through such channels, each percentage point of the unemployment rate boosts the federal deficit by roughly $25 billion. So a return to 4% unemployment would eliminate most of Ronald Reagan's immense deficits.

Fourth, we could stop the rip-off of public resources. Vast amounts of oil and gas are still produced in this country, increasingly from wells on federal lands or on the federally controlled Outer Continental Shelf. In place of James Watt's

eral major social services were examined in Chapter 8.
ecurity, the largest and most successful benefit program,
d additional funds in decades to come; but the retirees of
t century will impose no greater burden on the working
tion than did the children of the 1950s and 1960s. Health
a large and growing public expense, could actually be
er if it were socialized and made universal.

Means-tested programs for the poor—welfare, food stamps,
caid, public housing and others—too easily become mean-
ed, encumbered with bureaucratic (if not punitive) regula-
, and a focus for resentment among those who do not quite
ify for benefits. The better alternative would be to copy the
ular example of Social Security, and move toward simpler,
e universal benefits. Family allowances or guaranteed in-
nes could replace many of the specific welfare-type benefits
vided at present.

With the world's most productive farms, with storehouses
lging with surplus food bought by the federal government, it is
ard to imagine anything more outrageous than cutting back on
od stamps and other nutrition programs. The occasional "let
hem eat cheese" giveaways should be expanded into a comprehensive system of free distribution of some basic foods; purchases
for this program should be targetted to strengthen family farms.
Better planning of food production and distribution can, at the
same time, protect small farmers and feed the poor. The only
obstacle is the belief in the sanctity of the private market.

There are other services in need of reform or improvement.
Child care should be accessible to all families, whether or not the
parent(s) are working outside the home. People on disability
insurance, often severely injured or mentally disturbed, should
not face administrators who periodically decide to cancel their
checks. And the list could be extended. But the bottom line is
that, in a country with work to be done, everyone who wants a job
should be guaranteed one; and, in a country as rich as the United
States, everyone, working or not, should be guaranteed a minimum level of income—without the insults, obstacles and
harassment that often accompany social services today.

4: Democracy, Planning and Controls

The proposals described so far are quite similar to, and in
some cases directly inspired by, the books on economic demo-

giveaway program of resource management we could begin
charging as much as other countries do for private use of public
oil, gas and coal—or, like many other countries, form a public
corporation to develop public energy resources at a profit.

This is not a poor country! There is no reason to act like we
are penniless, as so much of Washington does whenever civilian
programs are being discussed. The economic tasks facing us are
vast—but so are the resources we possess.

2: Civilian reindustrialization

In decades past, industrial growth was based on the
international dominance of the U.S., on cheap oil, and on the
spread of automobiles and suburbs. Those bases of growth are
gone forever; a new direction must be forged, through conscious
planning and govenment action.

Many of the specific products on which U.S. industry once
thrived are likely gone as well: it does not make sense to rely on
the return of two-ton cars and eight-cylinder engines. But this is
not to say that services, technology, or information processing
are somehow replacing industry. We will still need to mass-
produce plenty of hard physical objects in the future—though
often quite different ones than we have produced in the past.

A policy of civilian reindustrialization will at once create
jobs and help rebuild the nation. Three areas in particular are
priorities at present: conservation and clean energy development;
public transportation; and inner-city reconstruction.

In energy, heavy use of any fossil fuel involves stiff economic
and environmental costs. Most of those costs are steadily rising,
as easy-to-get supplies are used up. The major commercial
alternative, nuclear power, is proving itself unsafe at any price,
with ever-more-expensive precautions failing to resolve either the
safety or the waste disposal problems. The Reaganauts' only
response is to wreck the environment in the hopes of making
energy cheap once again.

The better alternative would be to stick with tough environmental regulations, often to make them tougher, even though this
is sure to drive up the prices of coal, oil, gas and nuclear power.
The regulations are well worth the price: in exchange for higher
energy bills now we will be enjoying better health (and lower
medical expenses) in years to come; we will be preserving large

areas of the country for agricultural, recreational or residential uses in the future, rather than letting them be ravaged today.

Strict environmental protection makes clean alternatives such as conservation and solar power more attractive. Alternative energy efforts began to prosper in the late 1970s, spurred both by high fuel prices and by the Carter administration's modest programs in the area. Much more could be done; for instance, great energy savings could be achieved through such prosaic measures as weatherizing low-income homes in northern cities. In solar energy, photovoltaic cells which produce energy directly from sunlight are not far from being a viable private industry. Federal purchases of photovoltaics could provide the necessary push into large-scale, low-cost production, just as Pentagon purchases did for computer chips in the past.

Investment in public transportation both saves energy and makes crowded cities more liveable. A government concerned about solving the energy crisis would be repairing, not continuing to destroy, metropolitan and intercity public transit systems. For the many low-density areas of the country this means better bus service; for crowded metropolitan areas and heavily travelled corridors (such as Boston to Washington) better rail sevice is essential. Some of the most exciting new technologies for high-speed trains, being developed today in Japan and Germany, were invented in American laboratories but have never received public funding in the U.S.

The cities need more than better mass transit. Public housing, schools, parks and other facilities have suffered from years of neglect. Low- and middle-income housing construction need to be expanded. Streets, water and sewer systems need repairs; educational, medical and recreational facilities should be expanded. The software as well as the hardware of urban life has fallen into disrepair; education, child care and many other human services, mauled by recent budget cuts, need sharp increases in staff and funding. Community-based correctional and drug abuse programs could begin to replace the expensive and ineffective forms of crime control practiced at present. With such measures, the decline of our urban centers can be reversed.

In urban reconstruction, as in public transportation and in clean energy development, there are plenty of tasks that need doing, plenty of jobs that need manufacturing, construction and

transportation workers to fill them. C
along these lines would use our resour
needs.

3: Government with a hu

The emphasis on reindustrialization is
with adequate social services. There can be
doning those in need. Feeding the hungry, ca
disabled, providing education and recreation
nity and security for the old: these are th
economic activity, the mark that sets human s
the jungle, not some minor policy option that ca
because we're into tanks and tax cuts this ye
demonstrate what an inefficient, muddlehead
bureaucracies have often done in meeting huma
was not the underlying attempt to meet those nee
fault.

These basic human rights, then, should be affirm
to employment at living wages and decent conditions
who can work; and the right to security and social
those who are not employed.

A guarantee of full employment will not require
jobs. Civilian reindustrialization, and the restoration
services, will create more than enough jobs to be filled. In
our numerous public needs, the government should prov
at prevailing wage levels, or higher in the case of lo
occupations. It should of course pursue an aggressive po
affirmative action to open up traditionally segregated oc
tions (in public and private employment) to women and mi
ties. Many attractive proposals for employment policy
offered in the existing works on economic democracy, summ
ized in Chapter 11, and there is no need to repeat them here.

Full employment would reduce but not eliminate the nee
for social services. People employed at reasonable wages do no
receive welfare or food stamps. Jobs with flexible hours and
improved child care would allow some welfare mothers and
retirees to go to work. But there will always be substantial
numbers who do not feel able to work. People should be free to
choose to stay home and raise their children, free to choose to
retire at 65 or earlier.

cracy discussed in Chapter 11. Many people would doubtless find these ideas appealing but impractical. Wouldn't it mess things up to have the government play such an altered and expanded role in the economy? The suspicion is well-founded. An attempt to adopt a program of economic democracy would confront three major dilemmas: the inflation-unemployment trade-off, the threat of a capital strike, and the question of rising import competition. These problems must be addressed if the proposals made so far are to be viable.

Advocates of economic democracy sometimes point to the example of Sweden, the country which comes closest to embodying their ideals. Sweden has had extensive social services, steeply progressive taxes, and an unemployment rate under 4% for decades, yet it is a prosperous and clearly capitalist country. If Sweden's big businesses have learned to live with some measure of economic democracy, why not ours?

There is much to be learned from Sweden; in many ways it is an encouraging example. Yet its history is significantly different from ours. Its current economic policies have been built up gradually by a strong socialist party, which has been in office for most of the time since World War II, and by a labor movement which represents virtually the entire working population. In another country, an abrupt move today toward Swedish-style policies would encounter far more resistance.

Unfortunately, a more relevant example for us may be the problems encountered by the Mitterrand government in France. Coming to power in 1981, the French socialists set out to remake their economy. Workers were granted increased benefits and shorter hours, some major banks and industrial enterprises were nationalized, public spending was increased to stimulate the economy, and the government began heavy investment in French high-technology industries. The French socialist program of 1981 bore many similarities to U.S. proposals for economic democracy. (In Europe, supporters as well as opponents of such ideas commonly call them socialist.)

Within a year, the Mitterrand economic program was visibly failing. While the French socialists had made many moves that angered business, they had not gained public control over prices or investment. So they were still at the mercy of the nation's capitalists, who quickly counterattacked. Inflation mounted much faster than in neighboring countries. Private investment fell, and capitalists took their money out of France. Soaring imports and capital flight caused a collapse of the value of the franc. The government was forced to retreat, limiting wage increases, cutting back on its spending plans, and repeatedly devaluing the franc. By late 1983, even sympathetic observers were commenting on the decline of working-class support for the socialist government. The French èxperiment of the 1980s did not look like one which other countries would rush to repeat.

In the U.S. it may seem far-fetched for advocates of economic democracy to discuss what they would do after winning national elections. But the "Mitterrand problems" are real ones, waiting a bit farther down the road. What should we do when we encounter them? How would we deal with inflation, capital strikes and trade competition?

Within the confines of traditional economic policy, the problem with full employment is that it leads to inflation. Past administrations, particularly Democratic ones, have often professed interest in full employment. But none of them have stuck with it for long. In an uncontrolled, unplanned market economy, as explained in Chapter 1, businesses react to high levels of employment by raising prices; after all, their customers have a lot of money to spend, so the time seems right. Workers, too, realize that their power to win wage increases is greater when there are fewer unemployed people competing for jobs; and besides, they have to try to keep up with rising prices. Thus the great fear: prolonged full employment will send prices and wages spiralling upward.

The only traditional answer, for Democrats as well as Republicans, has been to cause a recession, to throw a few million people out of work so that inflation can be at least temporarily checked. Ronald Reagan has taken this route much farther and faster than his predecessors, but he is not the first to embark on it.

Another route to price stability must be found, if we ever hope to maintain full employment for long. But there is no other solution, within the limits of an unregulated private market economy; the only alternative is to control prices, to legislate the allowable rate of inflation.

Price controls are not a simple solution. They tend to become unworkable because of the way they interfere with the market. Freely changing prices, much as they are disliked by consumers, do play an important role in directing production. In a capitalist economy, even a monopolized one, price fluctuations are the signals which guide the decisions of businesses and individuals. If a commodity becomes scarce, its price will rise, inducing more production of the item; if this is not allowed to happen, a shortage could develop. In other words, imposing price controls on a capitalist economy will tend to lead to shortages of the items whose prices would have gone up.

However, price controls would also have immense advantages. The economy, freed of the need for frequent recessions, could remain closer to full employment. Formerly unemployed workers would gain the self-respect and security, as well as the incomes, that accompany steady jobs; production would increase; social welfare spending and government deficits would be reduced. High interest rates would no longer be needed to slow down the economy and control inflation; lower interest rates would boost construction and other activities dependent on borrowing. The advantages of finding some way to stop inflation without recessions make it well worth the experimentation and trouble which it is sure to involve.

Just as full employment leads to the need for price controls, the attempt to make price controls work leads on to the need for social regulation of production. Capitalists can always go on strike against controls, refusing to expand production at controlled prices and thus allowing shortages to develop. As the oil companies have been kind enough to demonstrate twice so far, sudden scarcities of an essential product like gasoline create an atmosphere of panic in which price hikes and other corporate goals can be achieved with ease. Capital strikes have proved much more reliably successful than their labor counterparts.

Any strategy that conflicts with the corporate agenda must be prepared for this scenario: controls or other inteference with business as usual can lead to shortages. It is not an insurmountable obstacle; it was overcome during our most successful past episode of price controls, in World War II. Those controls, like any others, created continual tendencies toward shortages.

The wartime air of urgency and common purpose allowed many unconventional economic measures. Direct government regulation of war-related production overcame many shortages; rationing and voluntary conservation to aid the war effort coped with other scarcities. When existing industrial capacity was inadequate to produce war materials, the government often stepped in and invested in new plants and equipment. By 1945 the federal Defense Plant Corporation had financed more than 2,000 industrial facilities, and owned more than 900 of them. Other government agencies provided aid to boost production of synthetic rubber and strategic materials.[2]

When there was a war to be won, no one waited around for private enterprise to perform. It was not necessary to use higher prices to bribe the economy into higher output. Could it be that our war planners found public enterprise a faster, more efficient way to get the job done? The evidence for this subversive conclusion was hastily disposed of after the war, as the publicly owned industrial plants were soon sold to private corporations at bargain prices.

As in World War II, what is needed today is public decision-making about what will be produced, and mechanisms for rapid movement of labor and material resources into new areas. The private market is too slow, too capricious, too beholden to corporate profit; some form of public planning is required. A national economic planning board should be elected, with the power to enforce the necessary levels of investment in and production of essential goods and services — either by regulating private business, or through the creation of new public enterprises.

Discussion of economic planning can easily become lost in the details of proposed planning agencies (this is the principal drawback of *Let's Rebuild America*, the otherwise impressive economic program of the International Association of Machinists[3]). The important issue today, as in World War II, is not the exact procedures used for planning, but the political commitment to reshaping production and investment. When the market is capable of withholding basic necessities such as health care, energy, or even food from millions of people, then the market must be overruled by some form of democratic decision-making.

Price controls and public planning of production, then, may be crucial forms of "economic democracy" required to make a reform program work. Among other advantages, such national-level economic democracy would gradually make it easier to create democratic workplaces and work relationships. But it is a mistake to pin great hopes on short-run gains in output to be obtained from workplace democracy (as is done by Bowles, Gordon and Weisskopf, in *Beyond the Waste Land*, the most ambitious of the proposals reviewed in Chapter 11). Like price controls, workplace democracy will probably involve a period of experimentation and turmoil at first. At all levels, from national planning boards to the factory floor, democracy is a desirable long-run goal, not a quick fix for the current recession.

The final structural problem to be addressed is the dilemma of import competition. As the Mitterrand government found out in France, moves toward full employment and higher wages in one country may lead to a rapidly rising tide of imports, as consumers spend much of their increased incomes on foreign goods while higher wages make domestic industry less competitive. And job loss due to imports already seems a serious enough problem in many industries today. How, then, would economic democracy handle the question of imports?

There are two principal answers. First, public planning would make very different decisions than private business about when to close a plant threatened by import competition. Public debate about the nation's long-term steel needs, rather than U.S. Steel's musings about the short-run profitability of getting out of steel and into oil and chemicals, would likely keep more steel mills open. As pointed out by Bluestone and Harrison in *The Deindustrialization of America*, the costs of closing a factory are much greater in public accounting terms (which count the loss of tax revenues and the increased cost of unemployment and other benefits) than in narrow private-sector profit and loss calculations. So public planning would more often keep factories open, or seek alternative employment for the factories and workers involved.

Second, civilian reindustrialization as outlined above would increase the number of intrinsically local jobs. Not everyone is threatened by foreign trade: construction workers, bus drivers, teachers and medical personnel, for instance, cannot lose their jobs to imports. An emphasis on energy conservation, mass transit, urban reconstruction, and improved social services would raise the proportion of the labor force producing non-tradeable goods and services. Production of tradeable goods will never be eliminated, but it need not be as central as it is today. This is not just a matter of replacing industry with services; blue-collar jobs in construction and transportation would expand, while some (not all) areas of manufacturing might contract.

The reign of the unplanned market is no more sensible internationally than at home. While reducing our vulnerability to job loss from import competition, we should also seek negotiated long-term trade agreements at stable prices, to insulate ourselves and others from the disruptive impact of rapid inflation. Gyrating world prices for oil, food, or manufactured goods can only wreak havoc with national economies, in the U.S. and elsewhere.

****

By now it is clear how to answer the question which has run throughout the last two chapters. Is economic democracy compatible with corporate capitalism? Or to say it differently, to name the name which terrifies so many Americans, when we talk about putting people before profits, are we talking about socialism? Certainly not in the most familiar sense of the term: no, we are not advocating the bureaucratic rigidity and militarism of the Soviet Union.

But in the sense of the original promise of the term—if socialism is understood to mean that our society's wealth, produced by our collective labor, should be subject to our collective control, and run for our collective benefit—then yes, economic democracy is one giant step along the road to socialism. If we are to solve the "Mitterrand problems," to cope with inflation, capital strikes and import competition, we will have to take several more giant steps in that direction. For private enterprise has shown itself incompetent to run a major industrial economy in the late twentieth century. It has proved, at more than enough length, that it is hazardous to our wealth.

The pursuit of something as radically unconventional as socialism requires a very long-term political strategy. Sadly, it is not likely to be won within the span of the 1980s, not likely to be the basis of a major presidential platform in the next few elections. While grassroots movements pressing for reforms are essential, as all the proposals for economic democracy have stressed, something more is needed. An explicitly, self-consciously socialist movement is needed as well, one which can articulate the broader vision of transformation. For the fact is that many important, popular reforms will upset the stability of the capitalist status quo. When that happens, there must be some voice in American politics, hopefully an increasingly legitimate and widely-heard one, which argues that it is capitalism, not the reforms, which need to be abandoned.

This has taken us far afield from the traditional boundaries of economic debate. Yet one step has led to another; there is no other road to an economy which works for the majority of us.

footnotes

chapter 1

1. *Atlantic Monthly*, December 1981. This article is also the sources of all later Stockman quotes unless otherwise noted.
2. See "Stalking Profits Overseas," *Dollars & Sense*, December 1981.
3. Ira C. Magaziner and Robert B. Reich, *Minding America's Business* (New York: Harcourt Brace Jovanovich, 1982), p. 225.
4. U.S. Department of Commerce, Bureau of the Census, *Statistical Abstract of the United States, 1980*, p. 648, and *Historical Statistics of the United States, Colonial Times to 1970*, p. 716.
5. *Historical Statistics*, p. 620.
6. The account of the size and composition of government spending in this chapter is largely based on "Big Government, Big Taxes," *Dollars & Sense*, July-August 1981, and on James T. Campen and Arthur MacEwan, "Crisis, Contradictions and Conservative Controversies in Contemporary U.S. Capitalism," *Review of Radical Political Economics*, Volume 14, #3 (Fall 1982).
7. *Boston Globe*, February 3, 1982.
8. These are December-to-December increases in the consumer price index.

chapter 2

1. George Gilder, *Wealth and Poverty* (New York: Basic Books, 1981).
2. *Ibid.*, p. 258.
3. *Ibid.*, p. 77.
4. *Ibid.*, pp. 99-100.
5. *Ibid.*, p. 28, p. 50.
6. *Ibid.*, p. 69.
7. *Ibid.*, pp. 114-115.
8. See the Census Bureau's *Statistical Abstract, 1980*, p. 354.
9. Gilder, p. 14.
10. *Ibid.*, p. 135, p. 131.
11. *Ibid.*, pp. 138-139.
12. *Ibid.*, pp. 51-52.
13. *Ibid.*, p. 252, p. 263, p. 268.
14. *Ibid.*, pp. 24-27.
15. *Ibid.*, p. 181.

chapter 3

1. *Statistical Abstract, 1982-83*, p. 431.
2. The evaluation of supply-side effects and references to the economic literature in the rest of this chapter are based on Campen and MacEwan, *op. cit.*, and on Robert Buchele, "Supply Side Economics Meets the Real World" (Smith College Economics Dept., 1981). Details of the tax cut and estimates of the revenue losses involved are taken from *House of Representatives Report 97-215*, pp. 196-292.
3. The extensive literature on this subject is cited in Campen and MacEwan, and in Buchele, *op. cit.*

4. The supply-side study is M.J. Boskin, "Taxation, Saving and the Rate of Interest," *Journal of Political Economics*, April 1978, Part 2. Criticisms of it are summarized in Campen and MacEwan, and in Buchele.
5. *Business Week*, July 25, 1983; *New York Times*, June 12, 1983.
6. Campen and MacEwan derive this conclusion, even if Boskin's controversial results are accepted.
7. *Business Week*, November 9, 1981.

chapter 4

1. *New York Times*, November 1, 1981.
2. *New York Times*, November 21, 1982.
3. *New York Times*, January 31, 1982.
4. Murray L. Weidenbaum, "The High Cost of Government Regulations," *Challenge,* November-December 1979
5. William K. Tabb, "Government Regulations: Two Sides to the Story," *Challenge*, November-December 1979.
6. *Ibid.,* interview with Carol Pierson, WGBH-FM, Boston.
7. Ruth Ruttenberg, "Regulation is the Mother of Invention," *Working Papers,* May-June 1981, and "The Gold in Rules," *Environmental Action, October 1981; Samuel Epstein, The Politics of Cancer* (Garden City, New York: Anchor Press, 1979), pp. 103-110.
8. *Business Week*, January 24, 1983.
9. *Ibid.*
10. *New York Times*, April 19, 1983, January 18, 1983.
11. *New York Times*, June 19, 1983.
12. *New York Times*, February 20, 1983.
13. *Boston Globe*, February 5, 1983.
14. *New York Times*, April 19, 1983.
15. *Boston Globe*, November 6, 1983.
16. *Statistical Abstract, 1980*, p. 217.
17. American Petroleum Institute, *Two Energy Futures*, 1980. This discussion of it is adapted from *Dollars & Sense*, February 1981.
18. Martin Tolchin and Susan J. Tolchin, "The Rush to Deregulate," *New York Times Magazine*, August 21, 1983.
19. Genevieve Atwood, "The Strip-Mining of Western Coal," *Scientific American*, December 1975.
20. *Boston Globe*, May 11, 1983.
21. Gail Robinson, "Gunning for the Clean Air Act," *Environmental Action*, February 1981.
22. Epstein, *op. cit.*, pp. 48-50.
23. Gene E. Likens *et al.*, "Acid Rain," *Scientific American*, October 1979.
24. George M. Woodwell, "The Carbon Dioxide Question," *Scientific American*, January 1978.
25. *Dollars & Sense*, March 1980.
26. *Dollars & Sense*, July-August 1980 and May-June 1982.
27. *Business Week*, July 11, 1983.
28. *New York Times*, March 2, 1983.

chapter 5

1. John Maynard Keynes, "The United States and the Keynes Plan," *New Republic*, July 29, 1940.
2. *Statistical Abstract, 1980*, pp. 372-373.
3. On employment from alternative prgrams, see Michael Edelstein, "The Economic Impact of Military Spending" (New York: Council on Economic Priorities, 1977). On the effect on manufacturing productivity, see any of the numerous articles and books on the subject by Seymour Melman; a handy summary is his "Looting the Means of Production," *New York Times*, July 26, 1981.
4. Iliac-4, the first of the current generation of supercomputers, was developed for and is still used for anti-submarine warfare, as described in Robert C. Aldridge, *First Strike!* (Boston: South End Press, 1983), p. 169. And since at least 1978, the Pentagon has been pushing industry to develop very-high-speed integrated circuit chips, more advanced than those sold commercially; see *Business Week*, June 14, 1982.
5. Military purchases from corporations were $60.9 billion in fiscal 1979. (*Statistical Abstract, 1980*, p. 372—this is the procurement total from table 604, excluding "intragovernmental" and "educational and non-profit institutions" procurement.) This was somewhat over 4% of the calendar 1979 gross domestic product of nonfinancial corporations (*Economic Report of the President, 1981*, p. 246.) Considerable anecdotal evidence suggests that the rate of profit is higher than average on military sales; the 8% estimate in the text assumes that the rate of profit as a percentage of sales in military contracting is twice the corporate average.
6. See, for instance, *Economic Report of the President, 1982*, pp. 85-87.
7. *New York Times*, April 12, 1983.
8. Aldridge, *op. cit.*
9. *Boston Globe*, January 18, 1982; *Esquire*, March 1982.
10. Philip Morrison and Paul F. Walker, "A New Strategy for Military Spending," *Scientific American*, October 1978.
11. *New York Times*, April 17, 1983.
12. For instance, see Fred Kaplan, "Rare Look at Flawed Air Defense," *Boston Globe*, September 11, 1983.
13. This discussion is based on the work of Franklyn Holzman, the leading liberal critic of the CIA statistics. His articles include "A Gap? Another?", *New York Times*, March 9, 1983; "Soviet Military Spending: Assessing the Numbers Game," *International Security*, Spring 1982; and "Are the Soviets Really Outspending the U.S. on Defense?", *International Security*, Spring 1980.
14. James Fallows, *National Defense* (New York: Random House, 1981), p. 50.
15. *Wall Street Journal*, February 17, 1982.
16. Fallows, *op. cit.*, pp. 35-49.
17. *Boston Globe*, February 7, 1982; *New York Times*, February 14, 1982.
18. *Dollars & Sense*, December 1981.
19. Paul F. Walker, "Smart Weapons in Naval Warfare," *Scientific American*, May 1983; Morrison and Walker, *op. cit.*

20. Walker, *op. cit.*
21. John Maynard Keynes, *General Theory of Employment, Interest and Money* (New York: Harcourt Brace & World, 1964 edition), p. 129.

chapter 6

1. Milton and Rose Friedman, *Free to Choose* (New York: Harcourt Brace Jovanovich, 1980), p. 141.
2. *Ibid.*, p. 141.
3. *Ibid.*, p. 215.
4. *Ibid.*, p. 223.
5. *Ibid.*, p. 106.
6. *Ibid.*, p. 137.
7. *Ibid.*, p. 13.
8. On physicians' earnings, see *Statistical Abstract, 1981*, p. 108; for average industrial wages, see pp. 396-398 of the same source. (Average hourly earnings were multiplied by 2080—52 weeks at 40 hours a week—to get average annual earnings.)
9. For example, Robert J. Gordon, *Macroeconomics* (Boston: Little, Brown, 1981), pp. 457-461.
10. *Economic Report of the President, 1983*. pp. 21-22.
11. Sidney Blumenthal, "Economic navigator for the Right," *Boston Globe Magazine*, April 3, 1983.
12. *Ibid.*
13. *Ibid.*
14. "But how long, you will say, is 'temporary'?...I can at most venture a personal judgment...that a full adjustment to the new rate of inflation takes about as long for employment as for interest rates, say, a couple of decades." Milton Friedman, "The Role of Monetary Policy," *American Economic Review*, March 1968.

chapter 7

1. As quoted by Senator Jennings Randolph in *New York Times*, April 10, 1983.
2. Proposed cuts in the WIC program have been widely reported. For proposed cuts in funding for hospice care for the terminally ill (virtually all for cancer patients), see *New York Times*, May 2, 1983.
3. *Wall Street Journal*, November 20, 1981.
4. For details, see my *Reaganomics: Rhetoric vs. Reality* (Boston: South End Press, 1982), Chapter 5.
5. The 1984 budget projected unemployment at 10.7% in fiscal 1983 and 10.1% in fiscal 1984; see *Budget of the U.S. Government, Fiscal Year 1984*, pp. 5-120. For 1983, 10.7% of the labor force was 11.8 million people. If the labor force grows 1% from 1983 to 1984, which is on the low side of recent experience, then 10.1% of the 1984 labor force is 11.3 million people. The 1983 projection of 11.8 million unemployed turned out to be too high, and if recovery continues the 1984 projection will be too high as well; they are used throughout this chapter, however, since they are consistent with the administration's assumptions embodied in Table 3.

6. *Ibid.*, p. 5-119. Despite the modest size of the projected drop in the number of unemployed people (see footnote 5), the 1984 budget assumed that those receiving benefits would fall from 5.4 million to 4.6 million—a declining fraction of the unemployed. And federal outlays were projected to decline from $36.9 billion to $28.8 billion, a declining outlay per unemployed person.
7. *Boston Globe*, February 15, 1982.
8. *The Nation*, February 5, 1983.
9. John Steinbeck, *The Grapes of Wrath* (New York: Bantam Books edition, 1969), pp. 384-385.
10. *New York Times*, April 10, 1983.
11. *Boston Globe*, March 22, 1982.
12. *New York Times*, June 5, 1983.
13. *New York Times*, May 1, 1983.
14. *New York Times*, May 27, 1983.
15. *New York Times*, June 12, 1983.
16. *New York Times*, March 7, 1983.
17. *Wall Street Journal*, November 20, 1981.
18. *Budget of the U.S. Government, Fiscal Year 1984*, p. 5-69.
19. *New York Times*, September 26, 1982.
20. *New York Times*, January 31, 1983.

chapter 8

1. *Boston Globe*, January 18, 1982.
2. *New York Times*, March 14, 1982.
3. *New York Times*, January 26, 1983.
4. *New York Times*, December 6, 1981, based on census data for 1978.
5. *New York Times*, January 5, 1983.
6. See the detailed analysis of the 1983 changes in Alicia Munnell, "The Current Status of Social Security Financing," *New England Economic Review*, May-June 1983.
7. *Ibid.*
8. As cited in James H. Schulz, *The Economics of Aging* (Belmont, California: Wadsworth Publishing, 1980), p. 11.
9. Although Table 5 is based on Census Series II-X, the same conclusion can be reached using Series I, II or III. See table sources.
10. The last two assumptions probably lead to an overstatement of the future number of dependents per worker. Immigration is likely to continue, and immigrants include a much higher proportion of working-age people than does the population as a whole. And a higher percentage of the adult population may well work outside the home in the future, since there will be fewer children per adult.
11. Schulz, *op. cit.*, p. 54, p. 63.
12. Magaziner and Reich, *op. cit.*, p. 20.
13. Robert V. Pattison and Hallie M. Katz, "Investor-Owned and Not-For-Profit Hospitals," *New England Journal of Medicine*, August 11, 1983. See also Arnold S. Relman, "Investor-Owned Hospitals and Health-Care Costs." in the same issue.

14. *Statistical Abstract, 1980*, p. 104.
15. *Dollars & Sense*, January 1982.
16. *New York Times*, March 31, 1983.
17. Mordecai E. Lando, "Prevalence of Work Disability by State, 1976," *Social Security Bulletin*, May 1979.

chapter 9

1. The third objection to the free-market labor theory is a brief summary of the arguments made by Lester Thurow in *The Zero-Sum Society* (New York: Basic Books, 1980) and elsewhere; see Chapter 10.
2. *New York Times*, September 28, 1982.
3. *Washington Post*, December 17 and 23, 1980; *Business Week*, December 29, 1980.
4. *Wall Street Journal*, February 12, 1983.
5. *New York Times*, February 16, 1983.
6. *Dollars & Sense*, January 1982; and information supplied by Dan Luria, United Auto Workers research department.
7. *Dollars & Sense*, May-June 1979.
8. *New York Times*, July 10, 1983.
9. *New York Times*, February 14, 1982.
10. See the summary in the AFL-CIO *Federationist*, May 14, 1983.
11. *New York Times*, October 10, 1982.
12. *Boston Globe*, March 5, 1982.
13. *Statistical ABstract, 1980*, pp. 428-430; NEA membership figures supplied by the NEA's Massachusetts office.
14. *Dollars & Sense*, January 1982; *New York Times*, December 27, 1981.
15. *Dollars & Sense*, October 1981; Richard W. Hurd, "Inquest on a Strike," *The Nation*, December 26, 1981. The *Dollars & Sense* coverage of PATCO was also based on Hurd's work.

chapter 10

1. Magaziner and Reich, *op. cit.*
2. *Ibid.*, p. 4.
3. Reich, *The Next American Frontier* (New York: Times Books, 1983).
4. Thurow, *op. cit.*
5. Thurow, *Dangerous Currents* (New York: Random House, 1983).
6. Felix G. Rohatyn, "A Matter of Psychology," *New York Review of Books*, April 16, 1981.
7. Rohatyn, "New York and the Nation," *New York Review of Books*, January 21, 1982.
8. Rohatyn, "Alternatives to Reaganomics," *New York Times Magazine*, December 5, 1982.
9. Rohatyn, "A Plan for Stretching Out Global Debt," *Business Week*, February 28, 1983.
10. *Business Week*, March 28, 1983.
11. High U.S. interest rates attract investment funds from abroad; and recession lowers our purchases of imports, improving the balance of trade.

The result is more money coming into the country and less going out, which strengthens the dollar. From early 1980 to early 1983 the dollar rose 40% against an average of major foreign currencies, causing a decline in the U.S. trade balance of perhaps $24 billion a year; see *Business Week*, June 27, 1983.

12. *Business Week*, March 28, 1983.
13. *Business Week*, July 25, 1983; *New York Times*, July 24, 1983.
14. *Business Week*, July 4, 1983.
15. *Business Week*, January 31, 1983.

chapter 11

1. John Maynard Keynes, "National Self-Sufficiency," *The New Statesman and Nation* July 8 and 15, 1933 (and *Yale Review*, Summer 1933).
2. Barry Bluestone and Bennett Harrison, *The Deindustrialization of America* (New York: Basic Books, 1982).
3. Martin Carnoy, Derek Shearer, and Russell Rumberger, *A New Social Contract* (New York: Harper & Row, 1983).
4. Samuel Bowles, David Gordon, and Thomas Weisskopf, *Beyond the Waste Land* (Garden City, NY: Anchor Press/Doubleday, 1983).
5. Arthur MacEwan, "Slackers, Bankers, Marketers: Multinational Firms and the Pattern of U.S. Foreign Direct Investment," (Economics Department, University of Massachusetts/Boston, 1982).
6. Carnoy, Shearer, and Rumberger, *op. cit.*, p. 157.
7. Carnoy and Shearer, *Economic Democracy* (White Plains, NY: M.E. Sharpe, 1980).
8. *Ibid.*, pp. 275-276.
9. Bowles, Gordon, and Weisskopf, *op. cit.*, p. 144.

chapter 12

1. *New York Times*, December 20, 1981.
2. Carnoy and Shearer, *op. cit.*, pp. 63-64.
3. International Association of Machinists and Aerospace Workers, *Let's Rebuild America*, 1983.